"Wow. Whether you're a theologian, a regular churchgoer, a nominal Christian, or just curious about this Jesus guy everyone is talking about, *Looking for God* will overwhelm you. It is remarkably profound, poignant, and insightful, and written with an uncommon and inspired sense of joy. I couldn't stop reading it. Amazing."

PATRICK LENCIONI, best-selling author of *The Five Dysfunctions of a Team*

"For years, Nancy has been leading seekers to a relationship with God. In this book, not only does she do that, but she also finds the seeker in all of us believers too, and leads us to finding more of Him. I recommend it!"

DR. HENRY CLOUD, best-selling author of *Boundaries*

"Nancy Ortberg's winsome reflections on the life of faith—and the struggles that inevitably attend that life—have been, simply, balm for me. I know I will return to this book."

LAUREN F. WINNER, author of *Girl Meets God* and *Real Sex*

"Nancy Ortberg shows her beautiful storytelling ability in these pages. Her stories range from funny to poignant and from gritty to tender as they explore the spirituality of elation, depression, normalcy, regret, sacrifice, teamwork, creativity, and more. Each story is like a clue in a quest for God, and through them, readers can experience what Nancy calls 'reconversion.'"

BRIAN MCLAREN, author/speaker (brianmclaren.net)

"Nancy Ortberg is not like Most-of-Us. At least she's not like the Most-of-Us that experts tell us we are supposed to be. Because she's not like Most-of-Us, she's got something to say to All-of-Us, and it is this: Most of us are not like Most-of-Us and it's okay not to be like Most-of-Us. Nancy's turned her wit and wisdom and rugged honesty into a new level of authenticity. Time passed me by as I read this book."

SCOT MCKNIGHT, Ph.D., author of *The Jesus Creed*

LOOKINGFORGOD

AN UNEXPECTED JOURNEY THROUGH TATTOOS, TOFU & PRONOUNS

LOOKINGFOR**GOD**

an unexpected journey through

tattoos, tofu & *pronouns*

NANCY ORTBERG

Tyndale House Publishers, Inc., Carol Stream, Illinois

Visit Tyndale's exciting Web site at www.tyndale.com

TYNDALE and Tyndale's quill logo are registered trademarks of Tyndale House Publishers, Inc.

Looking for God: An Unexpected Journey through Tattoos, Tofu, and Pronouns

Designed by Jessie McGrath

Library of Congress Cataloging-in-Publication Data

Ortberg, Nancy.
  Looking for God : an unexpected journey through tattoos, tofu, and pronouns / Nancy Ortberg.
      p. cm.
    Includes bibliographical references.
    ISBN-13: 978-1-4143-1332-0 (hc)
    ISBN-10: 1-4143-1332-2 (hc)
  1. Spirituality. 2. Spiritual life—Christianity. I. Title.
    BV4501.3.0769 2008
    248.4—dc22   2007036539

Printed in the United States of America

14   13   12   11   10   09   08
 7   6   5   4   3   2   1

*To my cousin Kenny,
who has been looking for God his whole life . . .
I love you like a brother.*

CONTENTS

11 12 13 14 15 16 17 18 19 20

ACKNOWLEDGMENTS

So many people have shaped, in such significant ways, who I am and how I see God—

My husband, John . . . you have loved me fiercely, and that has changed me.

My children, Laura, Mallory, Johnny . . . there is so much joy, there are no words.

And to a community of friends—Susan, Karen, Lisa, Rex, Elizabeth, Barbara, Marge, Dave P., Andrea, Jenny, and my mom—to name a few.

Finally, a very special thank you to the team at Tyndale, including Carol, Ron, Kathy, Lisa, Jessie, and Elizabeth. But especially to Carol, for working with this reluctant author.

AUTHOR'SNOTE

Everyone's story has a context, and mine is no exception. From time to time in this book you will read about a group called "Axis."

From 1998 to 2003, I was privileged to lead this ministry geared toward what we called "the eighteen to twentysomething generation" at Willow Creek Community Church in South Barrington, Illinois. Working on that leadership team with Steve, Heather, Daniel, Doug, Matt, and Jarrett was one of the most monumental eras in my life.

INTRODUCTION

I think I have spent my whole life relearning who God is. Usually I get it wrong. How could I not, with God being so big and all? Perhaps this is why we need eternity: One life is not nearly enough. Eternity is about the amount of time it will take to plumb the depths of this God of ours.

I don't think I am unusual (well, yes I do, but not in regard to this). No matter how great our parents were, how deeply we think or feel, how much we hear and read, we just don't get it right.

How *could* we?

He's God and I'm not, so the plumbing and learning and discovering continue. It's been a great adventure, though. Much to my surprise, God is much gooder than I thought. Of course the red, squiggly line on my computer just underlined *gooder* as improper usage, but I'm sticking with it. I spent such a long time thinking God was grumpy, angry, distant, arbitrary, and withholding. But since He is God, I figured I'd better just grin and bear it. How delightful to discover how mistaken I was!

There is a movie from the 1970s called *Soylent Green*. It stars Charlton Heston and is sort of a futuristic, bleak movie about what life could be like after decades of overpopulation and pollution. People live stacked up next to each other in dilapidated high-rises, and exist on a manufactured food called Soylent Green, since growing crops has long ago ceased. The dramatic surprise ending probably should have landed Heston an Oscar nomination, but it's another scene—before the ending—that has always captivated me.

In the movie, Edward G. Robinson plays Sol Roth, an old man who shares a tiny apartment with Heston's character, Robert Thorn. Sol Roth had been a man of letters, and his book collection is the only remnant of a kinder and gentler world.

In order to offset the dangerous and draining overcrowding of the world, the government offers an incentive for elderly people who volunteer to be euthanized. Before receiving the fatal injection, they will be placed on a gurney and taken to a room that contains a theater-in-the-round. In exchange for their lives, volunteers will be treated to a surround sound and vision experience of the world the way they remember it.

When Robert Thorn learns of Sol's intent to end his life, he races to the government facility where Sol is undergoing his final experience. Robert breaks into the room just as the screens are filled with magnificent scenes of a world set right. The only thing Robert has ever known is a gray world devoid of beauty. Now, with Sol watching in delight, he sees deer in a forest drinking from a stream and flowers exploding with color in a grassy meadow. He sees mountains covered in snow and the ocean crashing onto the shore, all set to the swelling strings of Vivaldi's *Four Seasons*. With tears falling down both men's cheeks, Robert Thorn shakes his head from side to side and whispers, "I had no idea. How could I have known?"

I love the wonder in his voice. I want to have that same reaction when I think of God. For many years, I thought things like longer quiet times would get me there. They did not.

I've fought hard to find this faith I've longed for, this God I've imagined. And I have found Him in the most unexpected places.

Surprises have clarified for me who God is, and I've found that challenging the prescriptive path has actually opened up the God of the Bible to me. As my understanding of God has grown, my faith has also grown—sometimes in ways that interfere with my life.

Annoying, yes, but also glorious.

This book is about the things that have sustained and propelled me toward God.

I had a lunch meeting recently with a man who goes to our church. He and his wife have just moved here from the United Kingdom and are launching an organization that connects churches with third world market products in order to help break the cycle of poverty. I asked him about his faith journey, and he talked about growing up in Christian circles and becoming increasingly disillusioned in his young adult years. Then, with great passion on his face, he described finding his way back, discovering this magnificently good God that he somehow had missed the first time around. He called it his "reconversion."

I understood completely.

1

THEPROBLEMWITH QUIETTIME

For most of my growing up years, I heard about the daily "quiet time."

It was revered and talked about as the bedrock of the Christian faith. It was described as a serene and profound time in the morning (anything less than thirty minutes was quite unworthy) when one sat alone with God in meditation and study over a passage in Scripture. It also included a time of prayer (usually following an acronym like *ACTS:* Adoration, Confession, Thanksgiving, Supplication . . . and we do not supplicate before we adore) and journaling.

After you had one—people always say they've "had" their quiet times—you talked about it. You might sneak it into a conversation in a way that was seemingly unpretentious, but always comparative. You'd talk about what a deep time you'd had that morning alone with God. How God had spoken to you. What a meaningful insight you'd received over a particular passage in the Bible. How long you had lingered over your journal that day.

And other people made sure to ask you about it in order to "hold you accountable."

"How is your time with God going? What is He teaching you?"

Quiet time was always the barometer for your relationship with God, the ultimate measurement of your devotion and maturity. It was as if your whole relationship with God hinged on that morning experience.

So for many years, I practiced my quiet time. Not quite daily, but close—and whenever I missed a day, I was filled with great consternation and guilt. Every day, I expected something profound to occur during my quiet time, but most days, nothing approached profound. And when I engaged in conversation with others about our quiet times, my experience never quite lived up to theirs.

Then there came a point in my life when for a number of years, "quiet time" wasn't an option. Now, you may disagree with that last sentence, but this is my book, and I am telling you, during that period I could not have done a quiet time if I'd had a gun to my head.

My daughter Laura was three, Mallory was only eighteen months, and I was pregnant with Johnny. Never was there a more oxymoronic phrase than "quiet time." In those days, I had to fight to go to the bathroom by myself, and when I did make it in there alone, one or both kids were always on the other side of the door, pounding and calling to me.

"Mommy, can we come in?"

"No."

"Mommy, when are you coming out?"

"In a minute."

"Mommy, is a minute up?"

I had never known before what it was like to wake up tired. Disrupted by teething and ear infections, my nights were staccato notes of sleep. When I woke up, the kids were either crying to be fed or unrolling toilet paper from the bathroom down the hall and wrapping the cat.

Days and weeks would go by without a moment for me to sit and open the Bible. And when those moments came, I either lost my train of thought or I fell asleep! But quiet time had been presented to me as the main/only means of connecting deeply to God, so I panicked. During this early stage of motherhood, I desperately needed God, but I was unable to connect with Him in the only way I thought counted.

I figured I could either meet with God again in about six

years (when all of the kids would be in school) or I would have to find other ways to connect to Him. And I did not know any other ways.

But God did.

I was standing in my kitchen trying to decide what to fix for dinner. Laura and Mallory were playing on the carpet but growing increasingly fussy after a long day. I was about twelve months pregnant, and exhausted.

I had an idea. We still had some time before dinner needed to be a reality, so I threw the girls in their car seats and headed off to the park, hoping they could work off some energy before I had to start dinner. (I also thought this could buy me more time to figure out *what* we would be having for dinner.)

I found a park bench I could sit on while the girls played, although I was so big I wasn't sure I would be able to jump up quickly if one of them needed something. I didn't really have a plan other than to let them play for about thirty minutes before heading home.

God's plan was to show me a window.

I watched as the girls dug in the sand and skipped around trying to catch the ducks. The sun was warm and low in the sky and provided me a sort of silhouetted view of my little redheaded daughters. I sat for a moment, relaxing into that scene, when all of a sudden I was so very deeply struck by how much I loved those kids. This wasn't just a recognition that I loved them but a very unexpected, visceral response. While I had been mostly frustrated up to this point, as I sat on that bench watching them play and squeal with delight, I felt as if my heart would just burst with the amount of love it held for those two little girls. I found myself fighting back the tears, feeling a tightening in my throat and an overwhelming sense of this deep emotion for my children.

Almost in that same moment, when my defenses were down and I was flooded with intense emotion, God sent a tsunami that absolutely blindsided me. He whispered to me, *And that's just the tip of the iceberg as to how much I love you.*

Now I realize that most people would be really grateful to have an experience like this, and they'd probably respond really well. But for some reason, my heart just didn't seem to have enough room to accept this message God was trying to give me. My mind didn't have the capacity to understand it. In that one sentence, there seemed to be more goodness and grace than my body could contain.

And it was simply too much to take in, so I said aloud, "Stop!"

I am sure more than one person passing by wondered why this twelve-month-pregnant woman was talking to herself at the park. Tears welling up in my eyes, I scooped up the girls, put them into the car, and drove home. Now, not only did I still have no clue what to fix for dinner, I also did not know what to do with this whisper from God.

When he wrote to the Ephesian church, Paul said he prayed for them that they might have the power to understand just how wide, how long, how high, and how deep God's love is (Ephesians 3:18). I find it fascinating that he should pray not just that they would understand the vastness of God's love, but that God would give them the power necessary to grasp it.

In the days that followed, that moment on the park bench would not leave me, and I found myself thinking about it often. Over time, I began to understand that much of my heart was Teflon coated. It was protecting itself from getting hurt, but in the process it had also became impervious to what it really needed. God had used a moment when I was most open to overwhelm and break through that coating with what my heart needed. God knew that I needed a deep understanding of the kind of love He had for me. But it felt so foreign to me that when I experienced it, "Stop!" was my first reaction. How funny to yell stop at what you most need.

The walls of my limited understanding of love had trapped me. But God cut a little hole in my wall—a window—and gave me a glimpse into the kind of love that He offers. Then He told me that it was just that: a peek. Nowhere close to the fullness of His love. And even the glimpse, at least initially, was too much for me. Sometimes windows are like that. We move rapidly away from what we see in them, only to be drawn back to the view.

I knew that I was not fully ready to comprehend the extent to which God had revealed His love to me that day, but I also realized something else. It had been a very long time since I had felt that deeply connected to the presence of God. There had been weeks and months of quiet times when I never experienced God like that. I had read verses and journaled about those verses and even talked with other people about those verses, but I had never been *that* aware of God. The encounter I had with God on that park bench went beyond any experience I had ever had during a quiet time.

God began to teach me that there were so very many ways to deepen my relationship with Him. So very many ways in which to know and experience Him. And that the park bench *counted* as much as the quiet time did. That was revolutionary for me.

Slowly I began to understand that I had been seeing God from such a narrow perspective. I had boxed God up and compartmentalized Him into thirty minutes each morning. But in reality, He had been waiting for me to realize that He had invaded all the parts of my day, if I would just pay attention.

So I began to have "quiet times" all over the place.

Not long after this, my husband, John, and I went to see the stage production of *Les Misérables*. Toward the end of the play, as the hero, Jean Valjean, is near death, he sings to his adopted daughter, Cosette, "to love another person is to see the face of God."

As I watched the scene, tears began streaming down my face. I am not by nature a big crier, so John quickly asked me what was wrong. I said, "That is one of the truest and most beautiful phrases I have ever heard. That should have been a verse in the Bible. Why didn't God make that a verse in the Bible?"

One night, a few weeks later, John got into bed and said, "I want to read you something."

He opened his Bible to Genesis 33 and read to me the words of Jacob, reunited with Esau after having been estranged for a long time: "For to see your face is like seeing the face of God" (verse 10).

I was so glad to see that God had taken me up on my suggestion to make that a verse in the Bible.

And after that, often when I was in conversation with a good friend, I would think that part of the experience was like looking into the face of God: a quiet time.

Whenever I ate a good meal, preferably one I did not have to cook, I was struck by the gratuitous nature of the God who made the colors, flavors, and textures of avocado, red pepper, and tilapia. He only needed to make food nutritious and caloric. Everything we eat could simply taste like bread and milk, and functionally that would be good enough. There is really no need for the variety and taste sensations that we experience when we eat, but God created them anyway. Steve Evans, a noted Christian philosopher, says that perhaps the best proof for the existence of God is banana cream pie. I think Steve is onto something.

So just as I found God in my friendships and in my children, I realized that a meal could also become a quiet time. Through my awareness of and gratitude for oatmeal with brown sugar, figs, and oranges, or mixed green lettuce and mushrooms, or horseradish sauce on a thinly sliced fi-let, I deeply reflected on the good nature of God. I truly learned what it means to "taste and see that the LORD is good" (Psalm 34:8).

We get so prescriptive with the spiritual life. We pre-package what it means to have quiet time, and then we duplicate it, mass-produce it, insist upon it, and brag about it. We make it a formula: Thirty minutes. In the morning. Prayer that includes adoration, confession, thanksgiving, and supplication. And then, of course, we journal.

I remember where I was the day I realized that Jesus never journaled. I was driving, and when that thought flashed through my mind, I challenged it. *That can't be true.* When I realized it was true—*Jesus never journaled*—I pulled my car over to the side of the road and couldn't figure out whether to laugh or cry.

I don't think journaling is bad. I just think we have come to see it as a spiritual necessity, and it's not. My husband is a pretty consistent journaler. It is very helpful to him in connecting with God. It is a practice that has helped shape his relationship and response to God. It is not so with me. I find journaling tedious. I am very self-conscious when I do it. I fall into the trap of doing it just to keep the dates consistent. I worry that when I die, someone will open those journals and notice the enormous gaps between the dates. John suggested that I pencil in "see other journals for missing entries," but I figured if I had to lie about my spiritual practice it might be time to find a new one.

I also don't think having a quiet time is bad. Quite the contrary. Quiet times have helped me enrich my relationship with God and transform my character. But when it becomes prescriptive and confining and routine, a quiet time can be more of a barrier than a help.

There are so many correlations in Scripture between the spiritual life and the life of an athlete in training. As followers of Christ, we need to cross train. Athletes do this so that the whole body is developed, not just a focused part of it. When we give ourselves permission to vary our spiritual routines, we emerge with a broader, multifaceted view of our great God. What a joy to realize that from the time we wake up in the morning until the moment we lay our head on the pillow to sleep, we have been given a variety of extraordinary ways to connect with our extraordinary God.

Not long ago, we were driving on the highway that goes

into Yosemite through the Wawona Tunnel. When we emerged from the tunnel, we came to a spot on the left where we could pull over: Inspiration Point. Scores of cars were parked there, and people were getting out of their cars to take photographs.

We got out of the car, and suddenly I was overwhelmed by one of the most magnificent views I had ever seen. The valley below was truly awe-inspiring, with El Capitan's sheer granite wall on the left, and Half Dome and Bridal Veil Falls on the right. There was no sign telling people to whisper, but intuitively, they were. It seemed that we were all in awe as we witnessed what can happen with a wave of God's hand.

As I looked down into the valley, I was reminded that a very big God is taking care of the universe. And all of this goes on while I am occupied with my simple little life. The beauty that He has created is absolutely breathtaking, and it is only a glimpse at the beauty of His Spirit.

And for me, it is a quiet time.

And it *counts*.

2

THIS, TOO?

As people who follow Christ, we have many places from which we can receive power and strength: prayer, Scripture, sharing with a good friend, music, solitude, or even the words of a great book.

But I think there is one power that we often overlook: gratitude.

My friend Nancy has a great life. She has a good job, and she really loves what she does. Nancy is married to Warren, and they love one another deeply.

On a crisp October day not so long ago, Warren and a very pregnant Nancy made their way to the hospital. Nancy had been in labor for about three hours, but since this was her first baby, she really did not know what to expect. Two hours later, after some pretty intense pain and pushing, Nancy and Warren met their 7-pound, 8-ounce, 21-inch daughter, Samantha.

As Nancy held her baby for the first time and reveled in the wonder of this new life, she looked up and said, "This, too?"

See, Nancy already had a good life. Not that it hadn't included a few hardships, but for the most part, she knew she was blessed. And as she looked down at Samantha, well, she was pretty much overwhelmed by this gift. With tears in her eyes and a heart overflowing, her response was simple gratitude.

It was a prayer whispered to God from a full heart that had just been filled even more. She simply couldn't believe there was room for more.

The power of gratitude is breathtaking and centering. It is along the lines of nuclear power. It makes our lives richer and fuller and freer. And it is a direct link to the goodness of God, which is an unending source of power and hope and faith.

Sometimes it's tough to be grateful. You cannot be a thinking person and fail to recognize the problem of evil in this world. Right now, John and I have a close friend in her late forties who is dying of a brain tumor. She has a husband and four children who are deep in grief and disbelief.

A man in our church, a physician with a young family, suffers from untreatable brain damage, most likely a reaction to high doses of chemotherapy for cancer, which ironically is now in remission.

We have another friend who has been battling breast cancer for more than ten years now. She is grateful for the extra time to be with her husband and children, but every day is a struggle. And her tired body is a constant reminder that the cancer is alive in her—held temporarily at bay by a combination of caustic chemicals.

The list goes on . . . a friend who lost a child, a friend whose marriage is painful and dissolving, a friend who was downsized out of his job, a friend who struggles with depression every day of his adult life. And this is just a glance at my small world. I haven't even opened the Pandora's box of war, poverty, hunger, oppression, unequal access to education and opportunity, suicide . . .

Without a doubt, the problem of pain makes it really difficult to feel gratitude sometimes. And plenty of brilliant people have written wisely on the subject from a Christian perspective (C. S. Lewis and Philip Yancey are two whose writings I'd recommend). The problem of pain always insists on the question, "Where is God?"

But there is a flip side, and not many write about this. What about the problem of goodness? What about all of the magnificent ordinary and extraordinary things that are a part of each day? That question insists on the exclamation, "There is God!"

Nature holds more beauty than our eyes can bear. Romans 1 says that even the earth gives witness to the creative power of God. And our response to that beauty—sometimes nothing more than inspired awe and reflective silence—gives witness and ties us to the incomparable goodness of God.

I was once at Malibu Beach near sunset. It was early winter, and the sky had begun to darken early. About a dozen people were standing on top of a high berm near the shore, where the stronger winter waves had built up the sand. I stood there with them as we watched a most magnificent sunset. We all stood quietly, as if we had purchased a ticket to a show and were now watching this grand display.

I wanted to shout, "You are watching God! You are attenders of one of His many shows that give clues to His goodness!" This sacred world.

Last fall we got a phone call about Mavericks, a point off the coast about thirty minutes from our house in Menlo Park, California. During the winter months, some of the biggest waves in the world hit at Mavericks—*big*, as in thirty- to fifty-feet big. When those wave sets come in as the result of a storm thousands of miles away, a call goes out around the world for surfers to arrive within twenty-four hours for the Mavericks surf competition.

Some friends of ours sponsor a spectators' boat that goes out during the competition to observe this spectacular event. So my husband, my seventeen-year-old son (who is himself a surfer but has promised me he will wait to surf the big waves until after I die), and I drove over the coastal hills to board the 7 a.m. boat.

At some point during the competition, I just paused to take it all in. There we were about half a mile offshore, looking back on the mustard-covered green hills that tumble down to the Pacific Ocean. Brilliant sunshine, seventy-degree temperatures, and crazy young men screaming down the face of monster waves on their boards. If the world gets any more wonderful than that, I am not sure I'll be able to stand it.

Those of us on the boat watched with a sort of reverence. We mostly whispered, although no one told us to. It was as if, for that moment, we were on holy ground.

Because we were.

Gratitude is a powerful force when I experience it in my own life, but perhaps the best testament to this incredible power occurs when someone who is facing deep difficulties expresses an authentic and profound gratitude.

I worked as a registered nurse for about ten years before my life took a different direction. One of my earliest patients was a young girl of about fourteen who had been in a dirt bike accident. I met this young girl down in the physical therapy department. She was in a whirlpool bath. I had read her chart before I went down to work with her and had learned that as a result of the accident, her leg had been amputated below the knee.

I couldn't imagine what it must be like to be a fourteen-year-old girl with part of your leg missing. I introduced myself and we made some small talk. Through the course of our time together, I learned that she was a follower of Christ, although she really didn't say much about that.

I was not prepared for her spirit, however, especially when she lifted her freshly amputated leg up above the bubbling water for me to see and said, "Look at how much I have left!"

She excitedly told me that since the doctors were able to amputate below the knee, it was much easier to fit a prosthesis. She wondered how long it would take to heal so that she could get started with that. I heard most of what she was saying, but I wasn't really paying much attention. My mind was fixed back on the "look how much I have left!" Her gratitude seemed really genuine. It wasn't denial or a Pollyanna mentality. She knew she was missing a good part of her leg, and she wouldn't have chosen that. But she was so very thankful for this bit of good news. Her spirit made my spirit soar that day. And I had two good legs.

Hebrews 12:28 says, "Therefore, since we are receiving a

kingdom that cannot be shaken, let us be thankful, and so worship God." Our gratitude, our thankfulness, is a way in which we worship God. We can sing, and that is worship. We can say thank you, and that is worship. And that day in the hospital, the gratitude of a fourteen-year-old girl moved me to worship.

Jesus, too, acknowledged that gratitude was a way to praise God. In Luke 17:11-19, Jesus was on His way to Jerusalem. Somewhere along the border of Galilee and Samaria, He entered a village, and there He encountered ten men with leprosy standing at a distance. They called out to Him, no doubt because they had heard of His reputation for healing, "Jesus, Master, have pity on us!"

In those days, leprosy was a death sentence. At the first symptom of this feared disease, people were immediately separated from family and friends and isolated with other lepers in dubious communities called colonies. So virulent was the spread, and so deep was the fear of this disease that those who lived in the colonies were required to shout out when any healthy person came within sight. So it makes sense that these ten men would shout to Jesus. But they weren't simply trying to warn Him of their presence. They shouted to Him for His pity. They thought that even His pity might cure them.

In this story, Jesus' response was immediate. He didn't tell them to bathe or put mud on their sores. He simply said,

"Go, show yourselves to the priests," something lepers did when they believed themselves to be cured.

As soon as Jesus spoke, all ten men were cured and released from the death sentence and the isolation of their leprosy. All ten.

Nine of them went home with very good news.

But one of them didn't go right home. The passage says that this leper came back to Jesus, praising God in a loud voice and throwing himself at Jesus' feet. *And he thanked Him.* Before he resumed his life, this man was compelled by gratitude to return to Jesus. And Jesus commended his reaction. Luke made sure that story was written down for Christ followers to read, so we don't forget to be grateful.

Dallas Willard says that if we are to find that this God we follow is not good, we should look somewhere else. Actually here is exactly what he says:

> The acid test for *any* theology is this: Is the God presented one that can be loved, heart, soul, mind, and strength? If the thoughtful, honest answer is; "Not really," then we need to look elsewhere or deeper. It does not really matter how sophisticated intellectually or doctrinally our approach is. If it fails to set a *lovable* God—a radiant, happy, friendly, accessible, and totally competent being—before ordinary people, we have gone wrong. We should not keep going in the same direction, but turn around and take another road.

God is so very good. In our busy lives, and in our preoccupation with what is difficult, we sometimes overlook the clues sprinkled throughout our day that are intended to remind us of the goodness of God. We forget to be grateful, and we miss the power in that gratitude.

I recently read about a man who became a Christ follower in his late thirties. He grew up in a home where God was never mentioned, and he spent most of his early adult years teetering between agnosticism and atheism—that is, whenever he bothered to think about it. Which wasn't often.

When he was about thirty-seven or thirty-eight, he began to sense a growing dissatisfaction within his spirit. Only it wasn't his life he was dissatisfied with. In fact, he knew that life had been pretty good to him. He knew he had many things in his life for which to be grateful. But this was the problem. He couldn't figure out who to thank for all those good things. Someone had to be thanked.

So this man went on a journey of sorts to figure out if there was some connection to this bursting sense of gratitude he felt and his lack of anyone to direct it toward. A few conversations, books, and churches later, he found Jesus Christ.

This man was so grateful that he finally had someone to thank. The right Someone. The Someone who was the source of all this good stuff.

He and that one leper . . .

James 1:17 says that every good gift in our lives has its source in God. That tells us a lot about the nature of God if we'll make the connection.

Once during an evening flight from Los Angeles to Chicago, I was leaning against the window trying to get some sleep. I had just finished a two-week speaking engagement in the Netherlands, Zurich, and Singapore. I was tired but energized at the same time, which is always a strange feeling. I was rethinking all that had happened during the last two weeks and feeling pretty grateful for the chance to be a small part of what God was doing in those places. The combination of speaking and being in those distant places had tapped into my deep love of adventure.

Interrupting all of these sleepy thoughts, the voice of the captain came over the intercom: "Ladies and gentleman, I wouldn't normally disturb you this time of night, but this rarely happens. If you look out the left (north) side of the plane, you will see the northern lights."

I had read about this phenomenon since I was a kid. Knowing I was interested in the northern lights, one of my children had even bought me a book about them, with pictures and everything. But I was not prepared for what I saw when I looked out the window that night.

Against a backdrop of complete blackness, thick bands of neon green lights danced and rippled through the dark sky. They looked like gossamer ribbons strung from the top of the universe, swaying back and forth for our entertainment. They were magnificent.

Much better than the book.

Everyone on the plane had moved to the left side to see the show. I was pretty sure the whole plane would fall out of the sky with that uneven distribution of weight, but it didn't. And in hushed tones, people oohed and aahed. Most of us were strangers, but in our mutual amazement, we were all connected, at least for the next few minutes.

And then, as quickly as they had come, the lights were gone. And everyone settled back into his or her assigned seat (properly redistributing the weight) and into our own separateness.

I sat in my seat feeling a deep sense of wonder. What a magnificent, gratuitous surprise. Even while I had been feeling grateful for having been used by God in my tasks, this gift pointed me to a laughing, whimsical God. A creative and interactive God who, in His creation of this wonderful world, decided that when solar particles interact with the earth's magnetic field, they might as well give us a show.

So whether we're looking out of an airplane window or into the faces of people we encounter every day, whether we're on the job or in our kitchens, whether we're reading a book or paying bills, if we will just look, we will see things that cause our hearts to well with gratitude.

God created the world, and it reflects His nature. Because

of that, we can see Him everywhere. And everywhere we see goodness, we see God. The only thing we have to do is connect the dots.

3

JELL-O

I SPENT A GREAT DEAL of time at my grandmother's house when I was growing up. She lived only three or four miles from my house, and when I got to be around eight or nine, I often rode my bike to visit her. I helped her rake leaves, tend to the many fruit trees in her backyard, and keep my great-grandmother company playing cards. Sometimes I even helped Grandma in the kitchen.

She had a busy stove, and about five or six bright, shiny copper molds hung on the wall above it. From time to time, Grandma would pull down the rooster or the rabbit or the four-leaf clover mold and pour a colorful warm gelatin liquid into it. She would ask me to open the refrigerator door, and then she would slowly walk the mold over from the stove top and slide it onto a refrigerator shelf. The next day at Sunday dinner, she would turn that molded Jell-O out onto a platter and garnish it with whipped cream. It was quite a sight.

Molds are fine for Jell-O.

But not for people.

What is it about so much of the Christian religion that insists people all be alike? Why do I so often feel as if they have their mold and they want me to fit into it? Do we somehow feel safer when others are just like us?

In John 21, we read about one of the post-Resurrection appearances of Jesus. After fishing all night, Peter, Thomas, Nathaniel, and a couple of other disciples had come up empty-handed. As they rowed their boat to shore in the morning, they saw Jesus standing there, although no one recognized Him. He called out to them, telling them to throw their nets out on the right side of the boat and that they would find the fish they were looking for if they did so.

When their nets were so filled with fish that they couldn't even haul them all in, Peter started to make the connection. This was Jesus—He had done this for them before. Peter was slow, but he was catching on. Close to shore, Peter jumped out of the boat so he could reach Jesus sooner.

Jesus had started a fire on the shore, and was cooking a

fish and bread breakfast for them. (Why don't we ever hear sermons about men cooking? We always hear about "what would Jesus do?" Why isn't this one included? I am not kidding . . . Okay, back to the story.)

After the disciples brought in their fish haul and ate the breakfast Jesus cooked for them, Peter and Jesus decided to take a walk along the shore. Most likely, this was the first extended conversation Peter and Jesus had since Jesus' death and resurrection.

Jesus used this conversation with His impulsive disciple to do a couple of things: clarify Peter's call and inform him about his death.

First, Jesus reinstated Peter. Peter would still have been struggling with the fact that he had denied even knowing Jesus following His arrest in the garden of Gethsemane. Here on the shore, in the rhythm of those three denials, Jesus asked Peter three times, "Do you love me?" Each time Peter responded positively, and each time Jesus followed by saying, "Then feed my sheep." Actually, the third time, Peter got a bit impatient with Jesus and said something along the lines of "Why do you keep asking me? You know I love you." To which Jesus quietly replied, "Then feed my sheep."

Knowing that He would physically be leaving the earth soon, Jesus was eager to clarify Peter's calling. He made it repetitively clear that He wanted Peter to shepherd God's people. In addition to that, in verses 18 and 19, Jesus gave

Peter a glimpse of his own death: "'When you are old . . . someone else will . . . lead you where you do not want to go.' Jesus said this to indicate the kind of death by which Peter would glorify God."

Then Jesus added one more "Follow me."

Most of us think that if we could just hear directly from God it would be easier to follow Him.

Really?

You gotta love Peter's response. After hearing directly from God, Peter noticed that John the disciple was following behind them, so he turned to Jesus and said, "What about him?"

What about him?

Peter had heard directly from God and as he paused to consider, he said, okay, that's what's behind door number one. I'd like to see what's behind door number two before I give my final answer. Not sure if this is a deal yet.

Peter wondered if maybe he'd rather have John's story. He wanted to do a little comparison shopping before he committed. What's so bad about that?

Well, you should hear Jesus' reply.

Jesus did not calmly reason with Peter. He was not sweet and nice. He did not try to reach a reasonable compromise with Peter. He was angry, and his response was terse.

"If I want him to remain alive until I return, what is that to you? You must follow me."

What is that to you?

Ouch.

It's quite telling that Jesus' response to Peter's desire to live another calling, another life, was heated.

Sometimes when I am giving a talk, I ask people to look quickly at the person on their left, then the person on their right. I say, "Do either of those people look anything like you?" Of course the answer is no. "Then why," I ask, "do you look to those people to try to figure out who you are supposed to be?"

But we all do it. And when we do, we compare the life of God right out of us.

The reason molds work so well for Jell-O is that gelatin is a substance without a form of its own. But people aren't like that, or at least we shouldn't be. Molds are rigid, predetermined boundaries that create shape but leave no room for movement.

Great for Jell-O, disastrous for people.

A few years back, I was asked to speak at a church retreat. I was scheduled to speak once on Friday night and twice on Saturday. After I gave the first morning talk on Saturday, the gentleman who had organized the retreat approached me.

"We have a woman from our congregation here this weekend whose story is quite compelling and seems to fit well into your topics. Would you mind if she got up just before your next talk and shared for about six or seven minutes?"

He went on to tell me some of the details of her story, and I agreed that her story fit perfectly. I told him I would be delighted to have her begin the session.

Somebody forgot to tell me the woman was Ketty Palau. As in Luis Palau's sister. Luis Palau, as in "the Billy Graham of South America."

Anyway . . .

Ever been in a room where the person speaking is so electric that it feels like the hair on the back of your neck is standing up? That you almost forget to breathe because you are so caught up in the energy of the message?

Well, that's what happened.

And I was so happy for her.

Except for the part that I wasn't.

I imagined everyone in the crowd holding up placards with big 10s plastered on them. Then, picturing myself getting up to speak after her, I imagined those signs plastered with 6.2s and 3.4s.

There was *no* way that I was going to get up and follow her. She was really good. She was brilliant, charismatic, and captivating. I was pretty sure that I was getting sick and needed to go back to my room to lie down.

Now you may be thinking that this was an immature response on my part, and I will give you that. However, you need to know that I have been a Christian long enough to know this is how it works: You're supposed to sin on the inside where no one else can see you.

So while all of those dark thoughts were swirling around inside of me, I made sure that on the outside I was attentive, nodding, and taking notes. I appeared as captivated as the rest of the people in the room. But inside, I had entered the world of comparison, and I was losing.

To my credit, I knew that something was desperately wrong with me.

Again.

So with the very few minutes left between the time when Ketty would finish and I would start, I began an inner dialogue with God. I thought it might be a good idea to try to get my heart in a better place before I spoke.

I imagined God whispering to me, *So, what, you want to be the only woman in the history of the Kingdom of God who can speak?*

Long silence.

Hmmmm. Well, I certainly wouldn't have put it that way, but since You did, well yes, sure, okay, if You say so.

Another long silence. This time I didn't hear God saying anything. I sensed He was waiting to let my response sink in to my own ears.

It did.

I didn't like the sound of it. Sure, at first I did, but after it settled, and I repeated it back to myself, well, it sort of left a bad taste in my mouth.

I suppose there was a part of my heart that really did want that. But it was a dark part, not my best part. In those few minutes, I faced something in me that I was not proud of, and I dug a little deeper to find something better. The part of my heart that did *not* want to be the only woman in the Kingdom of God who could speak. The part of my heart that wanted to be captivated by Ketty's amazing story, just like everyone else in the room. The part of my heart that wanted to be glad for her, for the way in which God had worked in her life and the way in which He had gifted her to communicate it so powerfully.

The excavation was successful. Once I found that part of my heart, I clung tightly to it as I walked up to the podium following the thunderous applause for Ketty and spoke the words that God had given me.

After I was finished and people started making their way toward lunch, I found Ketty. She had no idea of the internal warfare I had emerged from. I was glad of that. I stuck my hand out to shake hers and said, "It is a pleasure to be a part of the body of Christ, and to listen to preaching that is so obviously God inspired." And I meant it.

Comparison is so destructive. It erodes our love for other people and causes us to shun the gifts that God has given us. Like Peter, it keeps asking, "Well, what about him? What about her?" It keeps our eyes darting around the room, sizing people up, and holding up placards with numbers on them. It robs us of our own stories and gifts from God, all because we like someone else's better.

Comparison becomes a faulty scale on which we place ourselves, waiting to see how we balance out with the people on the other side. Comparison leaves us jealous and critical and insecure. It can propel us into unhealthy competition or relentless people-pleasing. God wants us free of that.

Part of what it means to be created in the image of God is that each person has his or her own story, giftedness, and calling. I cannot find mine by looking at yours. Your story may inspire me or warn me, but I should never use it to determine my own.

The gospel frees us from comparison, making it possible to admire other people's gifts and be grateful for their contributions to the Kingdom. In Christ, there is no need for Jell-O molds or rigid constraints. We are called to delight in the diversity that reflects the many facets of God and sheds light on what it truly means to be created in His image.

4

PRONOUNS

I ALWAYS HATED ENGLISH CLASS in high school. Let me clarify, I always hated the part of English class that was about grammar. I loved the other part—the themes and irony, the characters and their development, the writing and composition.

Grammar, not so much. I found it too detail oriented and tedious for my brain. While my cerebral circuitry was wired for stories, it slowed to a snail's pace when confronted with diagramming sentences and parts of speech. When I walked into English class and saw the familiar chalk outlines on the board announcing the autopsy of a sentence, I always groaned inwardly.

I never could understand how the same teacher who introduced us to such wonders as Victor Hugo and Jane Austen could show the same level of enthusiasm about participles. I struggled to stay focused as we slogged through adverbs and adjectives and things that dangled.

I was absolutely incredulous the day the teacher announced we'd be having a pop quiz on pronouns.

Pronouns.

Was she serious? At least nouns and verbs named things and declared action—but pronouns? They were like nouns' second cousins, twice removed. Who cared?

I have since changed my thinking about pronouns.

Mostly my thinking shifted when I began to better understand the concept of community. And a correct understanding of community has *everything* to do with pronouns.

Community is one of the most powerful concepts in the Bible. Genesis begins with it, and Revelation closes with it.

But we don't usually think of *community* as a powerful word. We've diluted its meaning, redefining it so that it's now soft and nondemanding—an unword.

Rightly understood, however, community is very powerful. It is God's people living together with God at their center. It is the way of life out of which evangelism and discipleship emerge. Community is where we learn the truth about ourselves, where we are deeply loved, where walls are broken down, and where people who are usually excluded are included.

When we learn grammar, pronouns seem like such little, inconsequential parts of speech. I know now that is not true. Much of the language we use to describe spiritual journey today is wrapped around the word *I*. It's a tiresome and small word, much too narrow to be used with something as grand as community.

Community has its own language. And when it comes to community, pronouns are everything. In community, first person singular moves to first person plural: from *I* to *we*. Somewhere my high school English teacher is weeping with joy.

In community, a deep solidarity with others can be found. In community, an identification and collaboration with others occurs. In community, it really isn't all about us. The kind of sacrificial, others-focused love that Jesus puts within our reach is reflected in the big word *we*. In using that pronoun, we move our focus off of ourselves and onto the bigger picture of others.

One evening, my oldest daughter came home from a Sunday evening worship service. She had been deeply affected by the experience and in response had written on a piece of paper, "Help me not to be okay just because everything is okay with me." I was so moved by what she wrote that I tacked that piece of paper up on our corkboard in the kitchen as a reminder that in community it is always *we*. In community, if someone else is not okay, then to some degree, I am not okay.

The *we* of biblical community points us to a kind of inclusion that is rare for most of us. In the highly stratified and separated social structure of Jesus' day, religious rulers and average folks did not mix. But Jesus demonstrated a radical inclusion that surprised the average person and upset the religious leaders. He spent time with fishermen, rabbis, Roman officials, children, synagogue leaders, farmers, tax collectors, women, and at least a couple of dead people. Jesus had a very big idea about what *we* meant.

In fact, in Luke 14:15-24, we read a story Jesus told that clarifies just how big His idea really was. See, there was a very wealthy man who decided to throw a big party and invite a lot of guests. While he was getting the party ready, he sent some of his hired help to deliver the invitations and bring back the RSVPs. Surprisingly, the assistants came back with forty-two noes and zero yeses. Apparently, everyone they had invited had offered excuses. Some pretty lame ones at that.

The rich guy who was throwing the party was pretty upset. He had expected that all of these people would *want* to be at the party. But since they didn't, and since this party was pretty important, he told his servants to go out and invite everyone they ran into. He told them to invite the homeless guys on the corner, the ladies who worked in the coffee shop, the guys at the bank. He even told them to invite all the people in the hospitals and nursing homes.

When that was done, and it was found that there was *still* room for more at the party, he sent his workers out again and told them to go out on all the roads and keep inviting. Then Jesus used this amazing phrase, "so that my house will be full."

In Jesus' day, the religious rulers would have assumed that God would definitely include them in His Kingdom. But according to this story, these were the people who declined the invitation. And that's when it went from *you* to *them*. Another fabulous pronoun shift.

Part of the surprise is that the Kingdom of God is made up of surprising people. And for our community to accurately reflect the Kingdom of God, we may have to broaden our idea of who to invite. The *we* needs to include *them*. Unsettling at first, but eventually expanding our idea of community to reflect God's.

There is an inclusiveness to the Kingdom of God that is unparalleled.

My friend Tamara taught me this.

Tamara and I were in a small group together when we were young mothers. We both had two little girls and were pregnant with our third child at about the same time. During the first few months of those pregnancies, we played tennis together about once a week. It seemed like a great way to stay in shape, but Tamara kept beating me and I found that annoying. So I suggested that we switch to going to lunch once a week. We shared a babysitter so our girls could play together, and spent our time getting to know each other better. We talked about God, our marriages, and our lives.

One day after lunch, we stopped by the library before going to pick up the girls. On the way in, I noticed a young woman out of the corner of my eye. You know how sometimes you see someone from that perspective, notice quite a lot, and make quick judgments? Well, in about two seconds I summed up that she was "white trash." Sorry to be so crass, but here's what I saw: She was dressed in clothes that were wrinkled and dirty. Her hair was matted, and she had a cigarette hanging out of her mouth. It was cold outside (okay, for California it was cold—probably 60 degrees), and her two kids were dressed in dirty clothes with no sweaters. One had no shoes. The woman was barking impatiently at one of the children and seemed angry and preoccupied. I didn't give her a second look.

On the way back out of the library, the woman was still standing there. As we passed her, we could hear that she was angry and yelling at her kids. Tamara stopped and spoke to her. "It's pretty hard when they're little, isn't it?"

The woman looked questioningly at Tamara, not sure if

Tamara was scolding her or identifying with her. She must have decided it was the latter, and almost immediately her shoulders relaxed. "Yeah," she said in embarrassment, "sometimes it's really hard."

Tamara spent a few minutes talking to the woman and learned that she was confused about how to find the nearest bus stop. Tamara insisted the woman and her children follow us to her van so we could drop them off.

Now while Tamara was responding like an angel, I was not. Oh, don't get me wrong. On the outside I looked great. Smiling, nodding, acting like I was thinking the same thing. But on the inside, I was a crazy mixture of anger and guilt. And I wasn't sure which one was going to win.

On the way to the bus stop, Tamara addressed the kids. "When is the last time you ate?"

"Yesterday."

You could tell the mom was mortified. Tamara quickly helped her recover and insisted, "We are stopping at Mc-Donald's on our way to the bus stop."

So Tamara and I and the mom and her two kids went through the drive-through and bought Big Macs and Happy Meals. Then we dropped them off at the bus stop.

It was weeks before I told Tamara that my inside and my outside had not matched that day. That her radical inclusion trumped my narrow-minded, first-impression judgment.

I've often wondered what that mom must think when she

reflects back on that day. She never saw Tamara again, but I have to believe she remembers the day that God's kindness and help intersected her troubled life through a woman named Tamara.

A woman who lived in the world of *we*.

Almost every time I go into my local post office, I chat with the guy who works there. We always have a fun conversation, and I often mention that he ought to come to church sometime. Last week he came to our church.

I greeted him, introduced him to some people around me, and sat with him during the service. For me, the most powerful part of that morning's worship time was when I realized who was on either side of me. On my right was the post office guy, and on my left was a high-powered lawyer who regularly attends our church. She had introduced herself to my guest before the service, and they had sat down on either side of me. They are from very different socioeconomic worlds. Except for dropping off a package to mail, this lawyer would probably never cross the post office worker's path. Except at a church.

What a remarkable place the church can be with the word *we*. What walls tumble down with the pronoun shift.

Jarrett Stevens, the primary teaching pastor at Axis, was a master of using the word *we* in his teaching. It made such a difference because it drew people together, making us feel like a community rather than a sea of individuals. I have often told Jarrett that he transformed us from a congregation to a community.

One weekend, Jarrett opened his message by asking for ten volunteers to come up onstage. He asked nine of them to stand off to the side and form a close circle facing each other. Then he talked directly to the one remaining.

"Your mission, should you choose to accept it, is to get into the middle of that circle in fifteen seconds. You can do whatever it takes to get in. Pushing, shoving, tickling, even drawing blood is okay." While Jarrett was describing the challenge to the guy, we could see the circle getting tighter. They began to talk among themselves and finally came up with the strategy of locking arms, touching legs, and slowly rotating in a circle to keep this guy from getting in.

During the next fifteen seconds, this twenty-two-year-old guy tried desperately to penetrate the circle. Finally, to the cheers of the crowd, he was able to push apart two bodies and dive in. He did it!

It took a minute or so for the ten volunteers to find their seats and the congregation to settle down. Then Jarrett spoke slowly.

"When I gave the instructions for this exercise, what is the one thing I never said?"

Silence.

"I never told the group to keep him out of the circle."

It's almost instinctive, isn't it? None of us would ever

intentionally decide to lock arms and rotate, but with the turn of a shoulder and the averting of an eye, we communicate to someone that he or she is not included. I did it with that mother at the library, and I'll bet you've done it to someone. The mom at the library wasn't the only person I have done that to, either.

I know you guessed that, but I thought I ought to say it.

I've excluded people, but I have also been the one excluded. A few years back I was getting ready to attend my thirtieth high school reunion. (My sixteen-year-old son said, "Why are you going? Everyone will be dead." I told him I was going on the off chance that one other person was still alive. Yes, he is a very funny boy.) Not long after I arrived, I saw Dana. Dana and I had gone to school together since first grade, and for a couple of months in high school she made my life miserable. Now granted, that was a long time ago, but I was surprised at the reflexive knot that formed in my stomach when I saw her. It was amazing how quickly I could recall the pain of that exclusion, and how equally remarkable that the experience had *not* kept me from doing it to others.

So often our instinct is to exclude.

The *we* of community is this radical inclusion that Jesus talked about. It is God's insistence that His house *will be full* and the declaration that invitations have gone out to people who weren't even on the original guest list.

Perhaps this pronoun shift is what the world is hungry for, the magnet that will draw them to the God who favors the *we*.

Funny how you can find God in a pronoun.

Who knew?

5
WORK

THE SUMMER I WAS FIFTEEN, I locked myself in the bathroom. Not for the typical reasons that fifteen-year-old girls lock themselves in the bathroom. There was no fight with my parents or disappointing love interest. I wasn't trying to hide tears or count to ten.

I had been working at my dad's company, Republic Supply, doing tedious, menial file work, when a woman walked up to me and handed me a white envelope with a little see-through window in the front. Being fifteen, I thanked her as though I had been expecting this and walked straight to the bathroom. I locked myself in the stall and as quietly as one can in an acoustically wired marble and mirrored bathroom, I opened the envelope and pulled out the contents.

I really had no idea what to expect. A letter telling me I wasn't doing a good job, perhaps? (Believe me, with my administrative ineptitude I was actually wondering why I hadn't already received that letter.) Maybe my coworkers were all very busy so they had put my next set of instructions in writing. This made sense, especially since it would sort of be like a scene from *The Man from U.N.C.L.E.*, and I loved that show. Maybe this company was a cover for a spy operation.

(Did I mention that I was fifteen?)

It was a paycheck. Typed and official. I must have stared at it for five minutes. To this day, that moment remains one of my most vivid memories, and you can check with my kids: I don't have many of those anymore. I felt a mixture of wonder, excitement, and pride. The check was printed on light pink paper with some soft wavy white lines. It was flat and crisp and slid perfectly in and out of its envelope. This wasn't Mrs. Atkins handing me some folded dollar bills after a night of watching her kids. I had landed on Mars, and I liked the atmosphere.

It wasn't just the paycheck I loved. It was work. I loved the feeling of doing something that mattered, something that helped other people, something that I could accomplish.

Growing up, I awoke each morning to the smell of coffee and the sight of my dad in his crisp white shirt and tie, sitting at the breakfast table reading the newspaper. The scent of his aftershave gently filled the room, and he always carried a sense of anticipation as he readied to start the workday.

Every morning my mother drove me to school. After she dropped me off, she continued on the few more miles to her workplace. In the 1960s, my mom was one of the few who worked. She was always dressed up for work, and her mood seemed to match.

Both my parents loved what they did, and they were good at it. That is a dynamic combination.

Thank God it's Friday.

I hate my job.

I can't wait until I retire so I can start living.

I don't get that.

Just as I did when I was fifteen, I still love to work. I love getting up in the morning and getting dressed for work. I love looking over my calendar to see what's ahead for the day. I love working with a team to make things happen. I love the relationships I've developed. I love the tasks. I love dreaming and imagining what might be, what the future could look like, and how I can make a difference. I love the process of change and improvement, and setting things in motion to make those things happen. I love celebrating the wins along the way and learning from the losses. I love watching the team getting healthier and happier as it gets better at the work it does.

When people are led well, not only do they accomplish great things, they also become better people in the process. There is that kind of redemption in work.

God gave work to Adam and Eve before the Fall. Work is not the result of sin; it is another way of working out the image of God that resides in all of us.

One of the reasons I think the workplace is remarkable is that it often brings together a diverse group of people who, in any other life setting, would never find themselves together. A few years ago, our family was vacationing, and the kids wanted to stop at McDonald's. As we waited in an incredibly long line to place our order, I watched as the manager of that McDonald's embraced his work. Behind the counter, the workers represented a wide range in age and demographics. I watched as this manager called out the best in each of his employees. First, he addressed a teenage boy who was grilling the food. "You're up to $7.25 an hour now," he said. "Do you remember last year at this time what you were making? I have never given pay increases that quickly to anyone."

The young man kind of blushed and looked down at his

feet. He said sheepishly, "Well, I've never really lasted at a job long enough to get a pay raise."

The boss said, "I don't even understand that. You've earned every single raise you've received. You've done a fabulous job! Okay, I need two cheeseburgers, ketchup only." And he was off to the next person.

An elderly man was working the fry station. He was probably retired and working for some extra income. The manager called the man by name, pointed to the fry station, and said, "Do you know what? Nobody does fries like you do. This fry station looks great!"

Next, he moved down the line to the ice cream dispenser, where a disabled man was pumping out cones. Again, he called the man by name and then made a terrible attempt at humor: "Boy, you've really got this job licked!" All the employees within earshot groaned good-naturedly in response.

But then the manager pointed to the man at the ice cream machine. "You have this cone job down so well, next week you start training with this man on the fry station."

The man on the fry station stood a little straighter, a smile on his face. The man at the ice cream machine stifled a grin, and it was clear they were both proud of their work.

But this manager wasn't finished. He turned to a young woman working the counter and said, "You know what? We've got to get you out of here. I know you've got to pick up your kids after school. Go ahead and go. I will clean up your station for you. In fact, if you want, bring the kids by for a snack on me after school."

She responded, "I've got a few more minutes. Let me at least wipe down the drink station." She wasn't leaving yet because he had earned her loyalty.

I was the most moved, however, by the way this manager talked to the middle-aged woman at the cash register. When I looked at her, the only word that popped into my mind was *lonely*. Looking at her grooming and clothing selection, I assumed that she was from that group of people often considered to be socially challenged. There was no jewelry on her hand to indicate she belonged to someone. I had the impression that in any other gathering of people, she would have been an outcast. But here she was at the center of attention, running the cash register, taking orders, and clearly enjoying herself.

More than once, the manager walked by and put a hand on her shoulder. He called her by name and said things like, "Four hours on the register, and you just keep these lines moving. I don't know how you do it." She, too, couldn't help but smile in response.

This disparate group of people was a team. Their manager was leading them and imparting meaning and significance to each of them. They were doing a great job too. What a terrific combination.

In his classic novel *One Day in the Life of Ivan Deniso-vich*, Aleksandr Solzhenitsyn wrote about the redemptive power of work. "Even with his body stretched to the break-ing point, he could feel a stab of pride when a gulag official looked over the row of bricks he had laid and commended, 'Good line.'"

We were created for work.

The average American spends approximately 60 percent of his or her life at work or doing work-related tasks. But for some reason, Christians think we need to separate our "work life" from our "God life." What we fail to realize is that work can be one of the primary places of spiritual for-mation in our lives.

It matters how we live Monday through Friday. Showing up to work with a renewed sense of purpose and the expec-tation of contributing both to the task and to other people plays a significant role in what it means to follow Christ.

Every day you go to work, whether that job is dead center on your passion and calling target, or it is simply a stepping-stone on your journey to figuring out what you really want to do, you have an opportunity to honor God. An oppor-tunity to tap into the joy of work and the joy of serving and the joy of leading. Every day you head off to work, you can join God in the adventure of that day, participating with Him in who He wants you to become and what He needs you to accomplish.

It is so easy to lose that perspective.

While I was attending graduate school, I worked as a registered nurse in a hospital in Orange County. I knew pretty quickly that this job was not at the center of my passion and calling, but there were many things about it that I enjoyed. And temporary or not, it was my job for the time being.

There were days that I went to work with a strong sense of calling and other days that I counted the hours between the time I punched in at three o'clock and punched out at eleven-thirty. One afternoon in particular, I had barely walked through the door before I was checking the clock to see how much longer until my dinner break. Internally, I grumbled my way through every patient I saw, thinking, *They could have handled this at a doctor's office. What are all these people doing here?*

I just wanted to go home. But, as often happens in an emergency room, two minutes before my shift ended, another patient walked in the door. I was told to check her in. I was not happy.

The woman was in her late thirties. Her three kids and husband had left for vacation the day before, but she had stayed behind because of her work schedule. She would be joining them the next day. She had been having some flu-like symptoms for a couple of days and was starting to feel worse. I made a note of her symptoms, asked her questions about her health history, and took her vital signs. All the while I was thinking, *You've got the flu, lady. Go home. I want to go home. Let's both go home.*

A short time after the doctor had seen her and ordered tests, her results popped up on the computer screen. Looking them over, the doctor's brow furrowed and he looked at me.

Leukemia.

Wow, didn't see that one coming.

She wouldn't be joining anyone on a vacation tomorrow. She would be transferred to the intensive care unit for monitoring, further testing, and consultations with a specialist. I looked into her face while the doctor was talking, and I saw the fear.

This woman had come into the emergency room with the flu, and she'd had to face a grumpy nurse who wanted to go home. Only the flu turned out *not* to be the flu.

She couldn't get in touch with her family until morning, so I stayed with her until she was transferred up to intensive care. I sat and listened as she told me about her husband, her three kids, her job. I answered questions and told her what kind of tests they would do, what other doctors she could expect to see. At one point, the tears slid down her face as the seriousness of her condition set in. She thanked me for staying with her.

The outcome of her condition was fast and ugly. She never left the hospital again, dying about two weeks after admission. I will never forget the sight of her three young children and her desperate husband at her bedside.

For me, it was a vivid reminder that every day I go to work I have an opportunity to copartner with God in what He is doing in this world. Not only when the job is in the center of my calling and passion. Not only when the job is doing lifesaving and revolutionary things. Not only when the job is in a church.

This past summer, one of my college-age daughters worked as a waitress in a nearby restaurant. I used to waitress when I was in college, so we had a lot of fun talking about her experiences. She had a fantastic manager who really motivated her to do a great job as a waitress. He often encouraged his employees to think about the people who were coming to the restaurant that day. He reminded them that some were coming while on lunch break from work, others would be meeting friends, and still others would be coming to celebrate. All were hoping that the food and the environment would be pleasant. Then he would tell the waitresses, cooks, busboys, and hostesses that they played an important part in that experience. He reminded them of the joy that comes from serving people. Yes, some would be difficult, but most would be reasonable people looking forward to their lunchtime.

Waitresses, auto mechanics, microchip creators, librarians, bus drivers, teachers, Web designers, coaches, venture capitalists, judges, construction workers, and lawyers—everyone has a God-given opportunity to accomplish meaningful tasks and value people in the process.

What a dynamic combination.

When our kids were younger, John spoke every year for a week at Forest Home, a Christian camp in the San Bernardino Mountains. The camp offered great programs for children, as well as loads of free time for families to hike, read, and swim together. Some of our kids' fondest childhood memories are of those times.

In the evening, while the kids were in their programs, the adults gathered for worship and teaching. On one particular night, just before John was to speak, camp director Ridge Burns stood up to make a few announcements. He had asked three of the teenage boys who were working in the kitchen to join him on the stage.

They looked a bit confused and quite self-conscious and awkward. They were still wearing the stained white aprons from the kitchen, but they filed up and stood next to Ridge.

Ridge began by telling us who these boys were and that they were responsible for much of what happened in the kitchen. Well, that was all he had to say to a room full of parents, grateful to have every meal placed in front of them for a week. The applause was thunderous, but Ridge quickly cut it short.

"Oh, I think there has been a misunderstanding," he said to us. Then he turned his back to the audience and faced those boys. He spoke directly to them:

"I didn't bring you guys up here for them to see you. I brought you up here for you to see them. Boys, the reason you are working here is behind me. I want you to look at all those faces. Those are the people you are serving when you are in the kitchen. You didn't have to come this summer. You could all be at home right now, spending days at the beach with your friends, but in choosing this work, you chose to serve, and these are the people you are serving. Let me tell you a little bit about them.

"They are parents. Some are married, some are single, but all of them have kids who are the most important thing in the world to them. They all work, some outside the home, some inside the home, and some work more than one job to make ends meet.

"They are delighted to be parents, but they are tired, bone tired. They get home from work and try to help their kids with their homework and get dinner on the table. They wonder nearly every day if they are being the best parents they can be. They are trying to connect with God but sometimes wonder how they can do that given how busy their lives are.

"This week they are here with their families. And you are giving them the great gift of time. I know, you thought you were giving them meals, but really you are giving them time. Because of what you do in the kitchen, they can linger over and enjoy three meals a day with their families. They can take hikes with their kids and spend time alone, talking and listening to God. They are being refreshed, encouraged, and filled—and part of that is because you are in the kitchen. Great job, boys, and thanks!"

I'm telling you, you could have heard a pin drop in that room as those boys started back toward their seats. And then the thunderous applause started. We were clapping for the boys. We were clapping for Ridge. What a great leader. What a great boss. What a great vision to remind a kitchen worker of the people he is serving. It's not about the pots and pans, the roast or the rolls. It's about the people.

We can easily miss the nobility of service when we get caught up in things like prestige, status, attention, and salary. Or in the unrelenting focus of our own satisfaction: Is this job my passion, my calling, my destiny? Those questions are good ones (except maybe the one about destiny—a bit overdramatic I think), but they are luxury questions. They are almost completely focused on "me," and we miss such a large part of why work is good and God-given: because it is not purely about me. Work is about serving.

I do like to think about the person God made me to be. I can get really caught up in discussions about how to live out of that person and find my calling and passion. But I realize that most people don't have that luxury. On Thursday mornings when the trash truck comes to our neighborhood, I wonder if the guys manning that truck are living out of their calling and passion. But even if they aren't, at least from a vocational point of view, it *is* still possible for them to work hard, serve others, and get joy and satisfaction from doing a job well.

There is something of the Kingdom of God on earth in that.

Work becomes one more place where we find God. There is not a nook or cranny in this world where God is not.

And nine to five is just one of those places.

6

ordinary

some of my favorite days are spent in my gray sweatpants and penny loafers. my husband tries to explain to me that you can wear sweatpants with tennis shoes, or penny loafers with jeans, but you cannot wear sweatpants with penny loafers. somehow that makes me want to wear the combination all the more, and it always surprises me that i have a husband who is part "fashion police." who knew?

in my gray sweatpants, i run errands, pick up the dry cleaning, buy socks and underwear for various family members, and stop by the grocery store. very lowercased, unimpressive stuff.

now don't get me wrong, i want to be as impressive as the next person does. but sometimes ordinary is just very nice. i called my good friend susan the other day, and she told me how she had spent the day in her garden. she talked about the various plants and the configuration of her garden, about the mulch and the work she had done with the hoe. but what struck me the most was the contentment in her voice. a deep satisfaction.

that day, susan felt deeply connected to God, and not because she was being still or slow but because it was such a lovely, ordinary day. nothing she had done that day was so remarkable that it would be written up in an article or told in a sermon. susan had simply enjoyed an ordinary day in this remarkable world that God created, and because of that, the joy and palpable sense of his presence were memorable.

ordinary can do that. it gives us a sense of purpose even in the mundane, a kind of freedom that releases us from the need to be important—a need that can weigh us down and sink us into our own pitiful selves. ordinary gives a peace and joy and centeredness that turns us toward God and builds him deep inside of us.

i grew up in a two-bedroom, one-bathroom house with no air-conditioning and a detached garage. i spent many of those days riding my bike, playing with the neighbor kids, and running into the kitchen through the screen door when it was dinnertime. i would easily use the word *ordinary* to describe my growing-up years.

delightfully ordinary.

what a wonderful word.

———————

bethlehem.

are you kidding me?

no four-star hotels or red carpet events. no book tours or conferences. but something was going on in bethlehem that isn't covered in the narrative. God had a reason for these humble beginnings.

certainly he showed himself often in the extraordinary, in the miraculous and breathtaking. without a doubt. but i wonder if we miss him sometimes because we miss how often the ordinary shows up—and the fact that God is there also.

and not just bethlehem, but through thirty years of obscurity. thirty years of ordinary days. thirty out of thirty-three. even the percentages are tipped toward the ordinary. what is there in that for us to understand?

sometimes when i am driving through a small town, i notice the laundry hanging on the clotheslines in the backyards and i wonder how many ordinary stories and ordinary days are lived out in that town, and around the world.

ordinary lives that can please and honor God.

when i was in my midtwenties, i spent a fair amount of time in the doctor's office being tested for what looked like a chronic, progressive neurological disease. for about four months, i thought i might be spending the rest of my life in a wheelchair. i remember thinking, *what i wouldn't give for the promise of a lifetime of ordinary days.*

over time, it became clear that whatever was causing the problem was not as serious as we had feared and that i would indeed walk through the rest of my life. what stayed with me after that was a deep appreciation for ordinary days. God is just as present in the days that all run together, days when nothing really stands out, as he is in the extraordinary days.

perhaps when we are looking for God, we neglect the ordinary; we are fooled into thinking that if it is God, he will be in the grand and glorious, in the defining moment, in the 180-degree turn.

certainly he is there. but not *only* there.

God is so great and so everywhere that even the ordinary is sacred. ordinary days, ordinary places, ordinary activities—he is there. even in my lowercased ordinary-ness.

that is a good place to go looking.

7

THEBWORD

I REMEMBER IT LIKE IT WAS YESTERDAY. I had heard rumblings about a balanced life, but I really didn't know how to achieve it. I had heard people talking about how balance changed their lives and how pleased it made God, but I didn't completely understand it. Then I went to a conference and heard a speaker.

He drew the pie chart, and I was hooked. It was so simple and neat, I wondered why it had taken me so long to find it. This was my answer, and I scribbled furiously into each of the evenly divided compartments in the circle. There were titles and Bible verses for each of the areas. When he finished speaking, there it was: my beautiful circle, my balanced life.

There was a section for God, and naturally He was the first section we all filled in. We needed to understand that to make this balanced life work, God had to be the first slice. Then came family and work and exercise and friendships, and then a host of optional slices (such as school) depending on your season of life.

There was such hope and promise in that circle. The answer to what ailed me. I embarked on my new life with an eagerness akin to being born again. There was just one problem. Actually, there were three.

It didn't work.

It wasn't theologically correct.

And, it wasn't all that much fun.

Let's take the second one first. You'd be hard pressed to find a person in the Bible who was noted for his or her "balanced life." Peter, who was one of the first to leave his chosen career to follow Jesus, just dropped his nets and signed on for life. Paul—you know where I'm going with this—opened his Blackberry calendar to show the Corinthian church his schedule, which included prison time, floggings, lashings, shipwrecks, and starvation. Paul was in serious need of a circle.

And Jesus?

Please!

He had to move away from the crowds because they had kept Him all day. He even ended up sleeping through a storm on a boat, He was so tired. Talked about having no place to lay His head at night. Not a poster boy for balance.

Wait a minute, you say! There was Mary (of Mary and Martha fame). What about Mary? Now *she* was balanced.

Except for the part that she wasn't.

Remember when Jesus spoke to Martha and told her that Mary had chosen the "one thing" that cannot be taken away? Well, at first glance, it might appear that Mary was moving in the direction of balance. But actually it was quite the opposite. Pretty much what Jesus was saying to Martha was "Mary is doing the right thing. She is rejecting the current social role for women, and rather than being in the kitchen, following her prescribed slices of life, she is sitting at the feet of the rabbi, learning like a disciple." That was a role exclusively for men in that day. Mary wasn't even *in* her own circle!

You can build a case for a lot of things from the Bible—picking up your cross, denying yourself, abandoning yourself to a good God, paying the cost of discipleship—but there aren't a lot of case studies on balance. The theology just isn't there.

A number of years ago, my husband went with a group from our church to Ethiopia. At that time we had two children, ages three years and eighteen months. I am sure those two little girls were on John's mind when he was serving in that greatly underresourced country.

I'll never forget his greeting when he got off the plane after being gone for two weeks. He grabbed me and the girls like he would never let us go. Then when we got in the car, as he was rehashing what they saw and did, he said, "You know, when an Ethiopian mother who's wondering where her child's next meal is going to come from thinks of American Christians, I doubt that she is hoping we'll learn to lead balanced lives."

Wow.

And anyway, beyond not being theologically correct, I'm just not sure balance works.

Balance is an interesting word that conjures up images of a gymnast concentrating all her efforts on remaining on that beam. Points are deducted for wobbles and missteps. And no matter how dogged her determination, there is no way she can last indefinitely.

Even at her best, her balance is only temporary.

Balance gives the illusion of control. The comfort of order. Many are drawn to the idea of balance because it promises to relieve the stress of our world, whose competing priorities are constantly clamoring to get our attention.

As we hurriedly try to attend to all of these priorities, we exhaust ourselves in the process, feeling unfulfilled, unfocused, and tired, and confused by a God who seems to want us to do so much.

So we draw our circles, looking for balance. And for a while, we are at peace. Then life accelerates, we try to squeeze a couple more sections into our circle, and once again, balance slips away. Our circle with its dividing lines has predetermined who and what will get our attention, leaving us unable to respond in the moment, needing rather to maintain our precarious balance.

One of the dangers of Christianity is that we often follow a concept as though it is gospel without really thinking through its accuracy.

I believe that balance is a myth. A unicorn. A pleasant story, a beautiful creature, but still a myth. Children who wake up crying in the middle of the night with a 103-degree fever and a strangling cough aren't looking for a balanced parent. They are looking for some medicine, a cool washcloth, and a song—all delivered by a mom or dad who makes the time to hold them chest-to-chest in the rocking chair until they are asleep again.

Work and leadership often require our full involvement or additional input that smudges the lines in our circles. Jobs that we are passionate about will require passion from us that is not neatly contained in any circle.

The people I admire most are those who live in full abandon to their God, to the gifts He has blessed them with, and to the goal of making a difference in this broken world. I watch them not only with admiration but with a deep stirring inside. I am drawn to live like that.

I think what God wants for us is a well-ordered heart. Not a circle with lines but a heart that is full of His love, spilling over into the lives of others. A life that is loving God with all of our heart, all of our soul, all of our mind, and all of our strength. And as a result, a heart that loves other people like we love ourselves. A rhythm of life that renews the life of God in us, that allows for mistakes and messes, joys and impact: a life no circle can contain.

One final thought: Part of the draw we feel toward balance is God's fault. He created such a marvelous world. The thought that I can grow roses . . . and lead a meeting where great ideas and strategies emerge . . . and study the history of Europe . . . and ride a horse . . . and get lost in the words and melody of a poem . . . and seriously consider what the economic forces of poverty are and try to help change that . . . and bake a banana cream pie and relish every bite— there are just too many wonderful things, so much I do not want to miss.

One life is not enough.

8
SHOES

SALT IS SUCH A SIMPLE THING, REALLY. Mined from the earth, evaporated out of the sea, sprinkled on our food. When salt is in its container, we don't give it much thought.

Imagine you are enjoying dinner with some good friends at your favorite restaurant. The food is wonderful and the ambience of the restaurant is warm and inviting. Best of all is the company of people you love. You tell stories from the past, catch up on their lives, and know that when you leave, you'll treasure the memory of this evening for a long time.

Insert one small detail into the story. When your dinner arrives, although it is good, you notice that the food is quite lacking in salt. You probably don't give it much thought before you simply pick up the saltshaker, maybe even in midsentence, and give it a few gentle shakes over your plate.

Of all of the memories you'll have of that evening, it's likely that none of them will contain the moment you shook the salt. You might perhaps remember tasting the food after that and noticing the improvement, but it certainly won't rank among the most memorable moments of the evening.

Sometimes God calls us to do great things for Him. Sometimes He calls us to get out of our comfort zones, get out of the boat, face the unknown, and do bold things in His name. The Bible is full of the stories of people in varying degrees of compliance as God called them to defining moments.

Sometimes, God just asks us to be salt.

The thing about salt is that it is never the main point.

It is not a defining moment. It is not a moment in history or of astounding greatness. But it is good. Especially to the one who is touched by it.

No one ever goes to a restaurant and returns raving, "You must go there! They have the most incredible salt I have ever tasted!"

The Bible doesn't tell us a whole lot about Mary the

mother of Jesus. We know a few things about her genealogy and where she was from. We know that she was engaged to a man named Joseph when God's angel told her of the divine conception of the Messiah in her womb. That's a lot of information to process as a newly engaged young woman.

The words that the angel used to explain to Mary why she was chosen are quite interesting: "You have found favor with God" (Luke 1:30).

He didn't say, "You will be the mother of the Messiah because God saw that you built a megachurch, you converted hundreds of people, you ran a successful business, and you are so beautiful." I think she found favor with God because of the way she lived her life. And I'm sure it was probably a rather ordinary life up until that point.

How amazing! In those days, Mary's life as a young girl would have involved mostly household chores and probably play. By today's standards of excellence and accomplishment, she wouldn't even register.

But by God's standards, Mary was found to be favorable. I think Mary knew what it meant to be salt.

In the Sermon on the Mount, Jesus spoke some of His first public words. First, He spent time explaining who He considered to be "blessed." And the list was somewhat surprising. Jesus said the blessed were the poor in spirit, those who were sad, those who showed mercy.

Ordinary people.

Then, right after those initial public words, Jesus said, "You're here to be salt-seasoning that brings out the God-flavors of this earth. If you lose your saltiness, how will people taste godliness?" (Matthew 5:13, *The Message*).

Of course, there are times when God does amazing things in our lives. Times when He asks us to do bold things for Him. We all have serious defining moments in our lives. But there is a lot of ordinary living in between those moments. Weeks, months, and years of life when we can honor God and reflect Him to a world that doesn't always see Him clearly—simply by being salt.

I recently heard the story of a woman named Sandra. Sandra volunteers with an organization called Project Homeless Connect. It was started by Mayor Gavin Newsom in the city of San Francisco. Every two months, in a large convention center, Project Homeless Connect provides a myriad of services for those who find themselves in need. People can receive dental or medical attention, free phone cards, eyeglass care, wheelchair repair, food coupons, and legal services, just to name a few. The first time the event occurred, over seven hundred people showed up. The last time they did it, over twenty-four hundred came.

On top of all that, the volunteers who show up come close to matching the numbers being served. When twenty-four hundred homeless people turned out, twenty-one hundred volunteers were there to help. When a person comes to the convention center, he or she is met by one of these volunteers who does a brief intake interview to narrow down which services the client most needs. Then the client gets a personal escort to the areas that provide those services. Gotta love the dignity infused in their service.

Sandra attended one of our church services to tell us about the role she plays in these gatherings. Sandra has a station that washes feet. When clients are brought to her station, she has them sit in a comfortable chair. Then she removes their shoes, if they have them. She slips their tired, swollen, blackened, and callused street-worn feet into a tub of warm water, brimming with Epsom salt and bubbles. Sandra washes and scrubs, clips and massages. She slathers on fragrant lotion as she asks them their names and their stories. After the attention they receive at Sandra's station, clients always leave with a new pair of socks.

Much of the gospel is about being salt so that we can help return a people who have wandered to a God who never left. It is about righting the relationship and restoring the world in its fallen condition to the way it was intended. Reconciliation can even be about a pair of socks.

With Project Homeless Connect, salt sometimes takes the form of legal services and dental work. It is as real and present in socks as it is in food coupons. The heart of reconciliation, the center from which it all ripples out, is Jesus. The act of His life, His death, and His resurrection makes reconciliation possible. And from there, every restorative deed or thought is a part of reconciliation. Richard Foster wrote that even the act of slipping a coaster under a drink is a move to "tidy up Eden." I love that.

Feet weren't meant to be tired or swollen or black. And every time Sandra bends over the tub she is a part of reconciling the world to God. Her actions will most likely never make the front page of the newspaper, but they don't need to. A little salt goes a long way.

———

Light is probably a bit more noticeable than salt. Being light, Jesus said, means being on a hilltop for all to see. It's about piercing the darkness and showing people the way. If salt is ordinary living reflecting the goodness of God, perhaps light is the defining moment that declares God.

One summer in Axis we worked on a four-week series called "21 C: How to Live an Authentic Faith in the 21st Century." As we put the finishing touches on the plans for the series, we really began to look forward to it because we knew it was going to be an exciting time. We had no idea of the light that was to come.

The speakers we had lined up were all Christ followers in their twenties who were living an authentic faith. One of those speakers was Shane Claiborne, a reedy, dreadlocked, winsome prophet who lived among the homeless in inner-city Philadelphia. Shane resided within a community of people who lived out their faith by building friendships with the homeless, acting as advocates in court, distributing food, planning summer art camps for the children in the neighborhood, and much more.

Shane told about the events that had shaped his life, starting a few years before. As a young man in his late teens and early twenties, Shane said he had been "shaken alive" as he read the words of Jesus. Almost as if seeing them for the first time, Shane's response was, "This stuff is crazy! What if He really *meant* it?"

As Shane pored over Jesus' words, he realized that Jesus talked more about serving the poor than about prayer and what it means to be born again *put together*. And he realized his life did not reflect that. So Shane decided to explore what it meant to follow Jesus by doing what it was that Jesus talked about so frequently. Shane toyed with the idea of spending some time with Mother Teresa in Calcutta, asking every nun in his hometown if she knew how to contact her. This idea caused some ripples of laughter throughout our crowd, but Shane explained how he continued in his pursuit until he crossed paths with a sister who actually answered in the affirmative. Armed with a phone number and the price of an international call to Calcutta, Shane dialed the number, and when someone on the other end of the line answered, "Sisters of Charity," he began to speak rapidly.

Shane explained that he was looking for Mother Teresa, and the voice calmly said, "This *is* Mother Teresa."

Yeah, and I'm the pope! Shane thought, finding it hard to believe that after all his searching, she would answer the phone. But Shane figured he didn't have anything to lose and explained that he would like to spend time working in the community. So Mother Teresa told Shane to come.

For almost a year, Shane lived and worked with the Sisters of Charity in Calcutta. He assisted them with the tending of the dying, with the cooking, and with the feeding of the poor.

Working side by side with Mother Teresa, Shane couldn't help but notice her misshapen and gnarled feet. One of the sisters saw that he was frequently looking at her feet and explained that once a year, they received a box of used shoes for the sisters. As soon as the box arrived, Mother Teresa took the box aside and removed the most worn of the shoes for herself.

As a result, Mother Teresa's feet looked like those of the most desolate homeless. Shane couldn't quite shake that picture.

After sharing that story, Shane opened the Scriptures and built the case for God's deep concern for the poor.

So much talk about care for the poor and so few churches that reflect that focus.

As we listened to Shane speak, those of us who led Axis

knew that the ministry we were leading was not aligned with that focus. Shane was so winsome in his proclamation of God's concern for the poor and our lack of it, that although he was kicking our spiritual behinds, we were all mesmerized by his vision.

Shane spent the last few minutes of his message telling stories of Jesus and how His heart broke for those who were poor and oppressed. Then, as Shane finished his message, he said, "Before we start singing, I thought a lot about how to end this. When this service is over, I will be going to downtown Chicago to meet some of your homeless. Then I'll come back and do the Axis Sunday morning service. At first I thought maybe you all could make some sandwiches for me to take downtown and distribute. But then I thought again about Mother Teresa's feet and the feet of the many homeless people I know. They really need shoes and socks. The street takes a terrible toll on their feet, so I was thinking that while we start worshipping, those of you who want to could just take your shoes off and leave them in a pile in the back of the room. I will take them down to the homeless this evening."

I'm not sure people completely understood what Shane was saying, so Daniel, an Axis staff member, said to our crowd, "Shane is not telling you to go home and then next week bring back a pair of shoes to donate; he is saying *right now* . . ." Daniel continued his explanation. He didn't stop at the words *right now*. But I did.

And for as long as I live, I will never forget the next moment. Just as Daniel said *right now*, the crowd "got it." All across the auditorium, the sound of Velcro straps being peeled back from sandals echoed.

Right now and the ripping of Velcro.

Isaiah 6 offers a great glimpse into what it's like to be in the presence of God. Isaiah saw the Lord in all of His holiness and goodness, and he realized the enormous discrepancy between God's purity and his own uncleanness. Isaiah's response was a confession of his sin and an immediate response to God's call: "Here am I. Send me!"

We were having an Isaiah 6 moment in Axis that night. Right there, right then, we were being asked to respond to God. Not later on that night or next week. Right now. Sometimes next week is just fine. That night was not one of those times.

And for the next twenty minutes as the band played worship tunes, we sang and we took off our shoes and we built an altar in the back of the room. An altar made up of twelve hundred pairs of shoes and a lesser number of socks. I wish you could have been there. We all have these amazing moments that never translate as well in the telling as they were experienced in the being. The feeling in the room that this was a defining moment was palpable. And our worship of God that night did not just consist in words that we formed with our mouths but in the removal of our shoes.

Here I am, send me. Well, at least take my shoes.

As people were leaving their seats to drop off their shoes, I walked to the back of the room. I wanted the whole picture in my mind's eye, and I watched as people streamed to the back to contribute to the altar. One guy in particular caught my attention. Joe was one of our group leaders in Axis, and I knew him pretty well. Most of the people walking back had their shoes in their hands. But he was still wearing his, and he spent almost the entire worship time walking around the ever-increasing pile of shoes. Finally, right about the time the music was wrapping up and the benediction was being spoken, he pulled off his shoes and threw them onto the pile.

A while after the service ended, I saw Joe and asked him what was going on.

"I came tonight very excited about what Shane was talking about," he said. "All through the message, I was completely hooked by Shane's words. Until he got to the shoe part. This week I bought a pair of 250-dollar rattlesnake-skin cowboy boots. (Now, why he bought a pair of 250-dollar rattlesnake-skin cowboy boots is for another chapter. A chapter that isn't in this book.)

"So I'm sitting there having an internal conversation with God while everyone around me is getting up in their bare feet to take their shoes to the pile. *You couldn't have had this in the service last week when I had my Walgreen's flip-flops on? You have to wait until I buy the most expensive pair of shoes I have ever owned?* I was pretty mad at God, but I kept singing on the outside so no one would notice.

"I finally figured that I at least had to go back to the pile. So I started making circles around the shoes. The whole time I was having this pretty heated discussion with God. Telling Him I wasn't going to take off my shoes."

"So," I asked Joe, "what changed your mind?"

"Honestly, somewhere between the third or fourth circle around the pile of shoes, this picture flashed into my head. I saw some homeless guy downtown in the Loop wearing this pair of 250-dollar rattlesnake-skin cowboy boots, and I started shaking my head and laughing. The boots slipped off pretty easy at that point."

The light was blinding. It penetrated deep into the dark recesses of our hearts, initially causing us to squint in pain, but then, as we relaxed and adjusted to the light, it flooded us, delighted and changed us.

By the end of the service the pile had grown to altar-like proportions, and the repercussions were just beginning. A small percentage of Axis attenders were young marrieds, some with children. When they picked up their kids after the service, they were met with the obvious question, "Hey, Mom, Dad, where are your shoes?" So a few minutes after Axis ended Saturday night, moms and dads brought their kids in to look at the pile of shoes and tell the story. Many of them knelt down to pray and to add little pairs of gummy shoes to the pile.

Right after the service, Shane and sixty Axis folks crammed into vans and spent the rest of the night handing out shoes. Someone even took the socks home, washed and matched them, and met the group downtown later that night. Those who went said it was a pretty profound experience.

The next day at our Sunday morning service, Shane did it again. Hundreds of shoes piled up in the back and were later distributed downtown. When that service was over, so many Axis people had to run quickly to their cars to avoid their bare feet being burned by the scorching asphalt. An older couple who had attended the main service noticed the unusual sight of people leaving church with no shoes. The husband commented brusquely to his wife about the inappropriateness of what he saw and actually drove by a group and rolled down his window. Before he could ask what was going on, a beaming young woman bent down next to their car and began spilling out the amazing story. She walked away as quickly as she had appeared, and when she did, the man's eyes filled with tears. He was embarrassed that his first response had been judgment, and he told his wife they were going to donate to the pile as well.

The shoes became a turning point in Axis—for individuals as well as for us as a ministry staff. We were deeply convicted by the discrepancy between Jesus' focus on the poor and ours. We had long, serious discussions as to how to turn this weekend into a lifestyle. We began by creating weekend serving teams that worked on a rotating basis with Habitat for Humanity, Bethel New Life (for homeless families in transitional housing), Feed a Neighbor (weekend meals for the inner-city homeless), and Youth Detention Facilities (juvenile prisons). One of those teams went out every weekend before the Saturday service. All of our home groups were asked to participate with one of these teams at least once a quarter.

At Axis, the shoes became the light that got our attention and showed us where Jesus was looking. Participation in serving the poor became a hallmark of our ministry. And the most amazing thing, while we were serving the poor, we were transformed.

That's light for you.

9

COULDWEPLEASE STOPTALKING LIKETHIS?

SOMETIMES I JUST CRINGE when I hear Christians talk. I want to scream, "No! That is *not* what I think. Please *stop* talking for me!" The way we talk matters, and what we say reflects what we believe. I think sometimes we just sound so incredibly goofy.

Not long ago, I found myself in a group of people who were not affiliated with any kind of church. About six of us—all from the same neighborhood—had accidentally run into each other just outside of a restaurant. We stopped for a few minutes and had a pleasant conversation.

Then just before she walked away from the group, one woman said, "I couldn't believe the parking place I got in this busy mall. God sure answers prayer!"

She was serious.

I was mortified.

After she left, one guy said, "Is she serious?" Another replied, "Oh yes. She's a Christ-i-an," making it a three-syllable word. After a round of snickers and eye rolls, the group dispersed.

Damage done?

Most likely.

How does someone talk about God that way and *not* have a negative impact? I imagine (and here I'll admit that I'm just speculating and may very well be sinning big-time) this woman later told her Bible study group that she had an opportunity to "witness" to her unbelieving neighbors. She probably even talked about her boldness and how she stood up for God.

I wonder if God cringes too.

We often talk about God as if He is this little blessing fairy, following us around and granting three wishes per day. We don't talk about relationship and knowing Him, or about our struggles and doubts, our wrestling and pain. Instead we tell stories of parking places that magically open up—and healings and miracles, ease and comfort, blessings and answers.

Sometimes we are, well, mindless. We do not acknowledge the work that faith presumes. We do not acknowledge the incredible struggle that many live every day. Instead, we gravitate toward easy, pat, naïve answers.

I know a woman in her early forties who had an unexpected and severe stroke. It hit out of the blue while she was at a meeting. She was speaking and began to struggle with her words. They slurred, then disappeared, and she slumped over in a heap and did not regain consciousness for nearly a month.

During that time, her friends and family prayed. They waited hopefully, and when she emerged from the coma, they called it a miracle. Maybe it was.

But I went to visit her in the hospital, and all I know is that if *that* was a miracle, God could have done better. She will never be the same. Her intellectual capacity is markedly decreased. Her awareness of those around her is functional but very fuzzy. Her body does not respond to what her mind tells it to do.

Her Christian friends clasped their hands and thanked God in excitement when she woke up. They told her how lucky she was, and then they went home.

For a miracle to really mean something, we need to use that word only when it really means something. Not to make us feel better about God. He doesn't need that kind of press.

Often the words we choose imply that God works for us. We wrap Him up in blue or red and claim Him for our political side. We tangle God and our political positions up so tightly, we don't see where one stops and the other starts. When our politics are affirmed through an election or a bill that passes, we claim victory for God. And when they don't, we claim persecution and vow to fight on. We never lose. But perhaps God does.

"You know that God will never give you more than you can handle." I have heard that one more times than I can count, but never in a more memorable situation than when a well-meaning Christian (I'm giving him the benefit of the doubt to make up for the overt sinning I think I did earlier) spoke those words to parents who were grieving the death of their child. I found it offensive that this person would say something so shallow. I was offended because not only does this statement *not* represent God accurately, it is theologically flawed.

I would also be offended by this statement if it were spoken about a job loss or a missed parking place. For starters, the verse that is derived from, 1 Corinthians 10:13, is talking about temptations, not trials or suffering. Beyond that, the idea implies that as followers of Christ, we are protected from heavy doses of difficulty. That is simply not true. This idea gives the impression that people going through rough circumstances have missed the protective shield.

Please protect me from that kind of love.

Of course we are going to face hard things in life.

Unbearable, unthinkable, inexplicable things.

And the power and the presence of God will meet us in those things. Difficult circumstances require from us enormous amounts of courage and faith that often come only after we've pleaded, searched, wrestled, and waited. Not as the result of a mindless and inaccurate phrase.

The way we talk matters. We need to think deeply about the theological implications of what we are saying and remember that God is not simply a useful tool to support our politics or our beliefs. He is not a pawn in our hands. He is not the parking lot fairy. He does not comfort grieving parents by telling them He knew they could handle it.

God is the powerful center.

For our soul and the souls of others, it is worth thinking before we speak.

Talk matters. The way we speak and what we say paint a picture of God in our hearts and minds. Not only do our words reflect our theology, they can also shape our theology. And what we say and the way we say it enters the ear and fires the neurons and deposits our concepts of God into our brains.

Theology is not simply thoughts or ideas about God—it

is what emerges from our lips as a result of those things. The way we talk about God has been shaped by our view of Him—and observing the way we talk about God can help us to check our theology.

Looking for God often necessitates struggle. It puts us in great company, with Jacob and Moses, Naomi and Peter. We need to be comfortable talking about tensions and ambiguities—knowing that faith is not the equivalent of having all the answers. We need to have authentic conversation that reflects our limited understanding.

An authentic telling may come years after the struggle, when we can sometimes wrap it all up in a neat little bow and present the struggle with the resolution. But we must make room for the words that emerge in the midst of struggle too, when there is no resolution on the horizon. Most people who are looking for God wonder if it's possible to have faith when we have doubts.

A resounding *absolutely* should follow.

10
JESUS

I HAD AN INTERESTING DISCUSSION with a friend the other day. We were talking about a mutual acquaintance, an older gentleman we both admired. After extolling his virtues for a while, I said, "Well, I know why I like him. Why do you like him?"

His response was quick: "Because he reminds me so much of Jesus." He said it in an almost surprised tone, as if he simply assumed I shared his reason.

I didn't.

"Well I like him a lot, but it's not because he reminds me of Jesus. Why does he remind you of Jesus?" I asked.

"Because he is always so nice and sweet!"

After we parted, I couldn't help but think about what he had said about Jesus. Was He really so sweet and nice? So I got out my Bible and a piece of paper. I drew a line down the middle and went through each one of the Gospels—Matthew, Mark, Luke, and John. Every time I found Jesus saying something sweet and nice, I put a check mark on the left side of the paper. Every time He said something that made me cringe—like "You're not worthy of the crumbs I brush off the table to feed to the dogs"—I put a check mark on the right side of the paper.

Can you guess which side of the paper filled up first?

Jesus was a lot of things. Sweet and nice aren't two of them.

Jesus was a walking defining moment.

Jesus was a catalytic mechanism.

Jesus' interactions with people rarely left them unchanged. He stirred things up and shook people's wrong ideas of God. He made heroes out of the most unlikely people and challenged thinking and lifestyles. He didn't end conversations by saying, "You're great just the way you are; don't ever change. Let's do lunch."

We want Jesus to be sweet and nice because *that* Jesus

doesn't require anything of us. But that's the problem. That is not the Jesus of the Gospels.

Unfortunately, those of us who have been following Jesus for a long time tend to think of Him as tofu. We don't really like the way it tastes, but we eat it because we know it is good for us.

But Jesus is really not like tofu at all. Jesus is actually like a Warhead candy. For those of you not familiar with Warheads, think of them as SweeTarts on steroids. The moment you place a Warhead in your mouth, your whole body responds, forcing you to decide if you can take the intensity or spit it out.

Just like a Warhead, the real Jesus shakes me awake to see that what God wants for me is so much more wonderful than what I am willing to settle for in the name of a "sweet and nice" religion.

In Isaiah 29:13, God's complaint against His people is this: "These people come near to me with their mouth and honor me with their lips, but their hearts are far from me. Their worship of me is made up only of rules taught by men." Then in verse 14, He goes on to say the solution is this: "Therefore once more I will astound these people with wonder upon wonder . . ."

Wonder.

That is God's prescription for healing from a religion of rules. I think we miss some of the wonder of Jesus because we have gotten so used to hearing the stories that we over-look the surprise punch in His teachings. Jesus came, and He stirred things up. He surprised people. He left the crowds openmouthed. He racked up ticks on the right side of the page.

In Luke 10, an expert in the law came to talk to Jesus. Well, actually it says he came to *test* Jesus. That could make a difference. He asked Jesus, "What must I do to inherit eternal life?"

Seems like a fair question to ask someone who claimed to be the Messiah. As Jesus often did when He sensed a question wasn't really a question, He responded with another question.

"What is written in the law?"

This expert in the law answered that he thought it all boiled down to loving God and loving your neighbor as yourself. He had probably heard that somewhere before.

And Jesus agreed with him. But the man grew uneasy; the text says he kept talking because he "wanted to justify himself."

"And who is my neighbor?"

It's as though this expert in the law had said, "If the last half of the answer is to love people, could you define *people?*"

Jesus realized that what this guy really wanted was a list of all the things he'd need to do in order to gain eternal life with God.

He was looking for a loophole. He knew he could walk away feeling justified if by *people*, Jesus meant *"certain* people."

So Jesus settled in to tell a story. But this story didn't include any lists; instead it reflected a boundless, open-ended lifestyle of unlimited and unqualified love for all people.

> A Jewish man was traveling on a trip from Jerusalem to Jericho, and he was attacked by bandits. They stripped him of his clothes and money, beat him up, and left him half dead beside the road.
>
> By chance, a Jewish priest came along, but when he saw the man lying there, he crossed to the other side of the road and passed him by. A Temple assistant walked over and looked at him lying there, but he also passed by on the other side.

Both men who passed by on this narrow path were religious men, having positions of responsibility in the temple. As Jesus was telling this story, the expert in the law was probably breathing a sigh of relief. A Jewish man, a priest, a Temple assistant. Yep, those guys were already on his list. He could love them. No problem. Yeah, he got that answer right.

But as Jesus continued, He said something that got this man's attention. The priest and the Levite both passed by. *Passed by.*

Didn't stop to help.

Could he be hearing this right? What's going on? Not only did these respected leaders in the Temple not stop, they both "passed by on the other side."

Now the expert was confused. How could they have passed by on the other side on the road to Jericho? There *was* no "other side." It was a narrow path, not a road. Everyone knew that.

Where was Jesus going with this? He was like a Jewish O. Henry. The expert in the law was probably getting a little hot under the collar at this point. Shifting nervously. *Passed by, you say?*

Then a despised Samaritan came . . .

Did He say a Samaritan? Uh-oh. That expert in the law, I'll bet he was *really* sorry he started this conversation and by now was probably wishing he could just thank Jesus for His time and end this.

Then a despised Samaritan came along, and when he saw the man, he felt deep pity. Kneeling beside him, the Samaritan soothed his wounds with medicine and bandaged them. Then he put the man on his own donkey and took him to an inn, where he took care of him.

The next day he handed the innkeeper two pieces of

silver and told him to take care of the man. "If his bill runs higher than that," he said, "I'll pay the difference the next time I am here."

The Samaritan, so reviled by the Jewish people and such an object of scorn and racial profiling, stopped. And before he stopped, Jesus said, he had compassion on this beaten Jewish man.

He stopped. He moved toward him. He bandaged his wounds, pouring oil and wine over them to soothe and disinfect.

He lifted the man and put him on his donkey, walking through this same wilderness, on this same narrow road where the bandits that attacked the victim may still have lurked.

He took him to a nearby inn and took care of him at that inn. He paid out of his own pocket for the victim's care at the inn. And he promised to return, paying for whatever wasn't covered in his initial payment.

Whew.

Ouch.

When Jesus told this story, He really poured it on when He got to the hero. The hero who just happened to be a Samaritan. And although the story almost speaks for itself, Jesus couldn't help returning to the man's question. "Which of these three would you say was a neighbor to the man who was attacked by bandits?"

The expert in the law had been looking for a list—the people he had to love in order to achieve righteousness by his own efforts. Instead, Jesus painted a picture to show him what his neighbor looks like.

And by the end of the story, the expert had no option but to respond to Jesus' final question by saying, "The one who showed him mercy."

And Jesus said, "Go and do the same."

No, Jesus is certainly not tofu.

11

COULDA, SHOULDA, WOULDA

BEFORE OUR FAMILY MOVED TO CHICAGO, I worked part-time at a home health agency in Los Angeles. I spent my hours driving to the homes of patients, checking to make sure that they were doing well and that our nurses and aides were giving the proper care. We covered a wide district in the Los Angeles area, and in the course of a day, I might find myself in a multimillion-dollar home, a middle-class ranch, and a run-down one-bedroom apartment. But although the outsides could be so different, what was behind the doors was always the same: people whose physical conditions were serious enough that their lives had been radically altered.

One Tuesday afternoon I left the office with my files in hand and drove to Baldwin Park. The address I was looking for was in a lower economic neighborhood, and most of the houses were pretty ramshackle, so I was surprised when I pulled up to find a modest, well-kept house, with a small but lovely garden in the front. I sat in my car for a few moments rereading the chart to make sure I knew what I needed to before going in. The family had recently emigrated from Mexico, so I knew they probably had little support in terms of extended family members or longtime friends. There was a husband and wife and two little boys, seven and three years old. The seven-year-old had been diagnosed with adrenoleukodystrophy (the topic of the movie *Lorenzo's Oil*) approximately two years earlier.

Adrenoleukodystrophy is genetic and fatal.

The mother answered the door and invited me into the living room, where her seven-year-old son lay on the couch. He was very thin, wore a diaper, and had a feeding tube in his nose. His body was skeletal, contracted in the fetal position. He was unable to communicate in any way, except for a soft groan he emitted every so often. In broken English, his mother told me that the doctor believed he was most likely blind and deaf at this point. Touch was the last available means of communication she had with her firstborn son.

It is one thing to work with an adult patient, but it is completely different when the patient is a child. The sight of that little boy on his couch-bed shook my composure for a moment. The boy's mother offered me a cup of tea, so as the three-year-old played with toys on the floor at our feet, we sat at the kitchen table to talk.

In my very limited Spanish, I asked the mother about her son's treatment and care. She took me to a cupboard to show me his medications, and I noticed that other than various bottles of medicine, the shelves were practically bare. It was a pretty bleak situation: The house contained very little furniture, very little food. My heart was heavy for this mother, new to this country, with very few resources, left to care for her terminally ill son. I couldn't even imagine.

I asked if she had any friends who might be able to provide some additional help for her. She quietly replied that she knew few people, and the ones that she did know weren't really able to help out with her son's complicated care. Their insurance only provided eight hours of nursing care a week, which was divided into two four-hour shifts. I asked about her husband's availability to help, and she became very quiet. The quiet never turned into an answer, so I simply repeated my question.

Hesitantly, she told me that three weeks earlier, her husband had left her. I was confused, sure I had misunderstood her.

"Do you mean he has gone out of town?" I asked. No,

she said, he had left her. He had told her he didn't want to be married to her anymore.

Three weeks earlier, they had taken their son for his doctor's appointment. With his diagnosis, these appointments were never easy, but this visit was particularly difficult. The doctor told them that as best as he could determine, their son probably had about six weeks to live.

At the most.

They weren't surprised by this news, just reminded again how sad their world had become.

Then the doctor said he wanted to talk with them about something else. The genetic test results had just come back on their three-year-old son. He, too, carried the gene for adrenoleukodystrophy. He would most likely come down with his first symptoms of the disease within the next year.

This was more than the mother could bear, and she wept. It was more than the father could bear, and he left.

And now, that mother was left virtually alone to care for her seven-year-old son in the end stages of a disease that had robbed him of everything it means to be a person. She would bathe and diaper, sing to and rock this child of hers. And then one day, probably in the next few weeks, she would scoop him up off the couch that had been his bed for the past year and place him in his little coffin.

And then, she would scoop her three-year-old son off the floor where he played and make a bed for him on that couch. And for the next few years she would bathe and diaper, sing to and rock that second child of hers. Until one day . . .

For me it was like a nightmare unfolding. For that mother, with all of her hopes and dreams for her boys, it must have been like waking up to find that nightmare was her life. It was just unthinkable, all of it, the disease, the father, the disease again.

Her aloneness, utter aloneness.

Those who know me know that I am not an overly emotional person. On the Myers-Briggs personality inventory I tend to be a "thinker" rather than a "feeler." When faced with difficult situations, I instinctively move into action mode. But as I tried to absorb all the realities of this woman's world, I had no answers. The only thing I felt was overwhelming sadness and pain.

As a home health nurse, I had seen a lot of desperate situations. I had never encountered something like this. I felt confused and stunned, and I had no idea how to respond.

I glanced over at the boy on the couch as the enormity of it all settled in, and I had the strong sensation that I needed to wrap up this visit and leave. It was as if some driving force were pushing me out the door, away from this impossible tragedy.

I finished up our conversation as professionally as I could. I told her I would communicate with the nurse in charge of her case and thanked her for the tea. I told her that she was doing a good job taking care of her sick boy. She smiled. I tousled the hair of the three-year-old still playing on the floor and walked to my car.

Almost on autopilot I started the car and drove just around the block, out of view of the house. Then I pulled over to the curb, shut off the engine, and just sat. And slowly the tears came. No sobs, although that would certainly have been understandable, just tears and a deep ache in my chest.

After a few minutes, my "thinker" kicked in, and I wiped my face with the back of my hand. I fumbled through my files and paperwork looking for a blank piece of paper. Then I started writing. I had ideas. I could help. Others could too, and I knew a lot of people who would be more than willing. Beyond tears I knew there were things that could be done, things that could make a difference. I was beginning to connect God in my thinking to what was going on in this situation. I could be a part of sharing the burden that the mother had been shouldering. There was so much that could be done. Before I knew it, I had filled the paper with ideas such as babysitting, meal preparation, grocery and gasoline gift certificates, housecleaning, and yard work assistance. Nothing could take away the pain of losing two children, but help could ease some of the difficulty.

It felt great to connect compassion and action. The presence of God in this world, in the face of so much pain, *has* to mean something. It could be a powerful force in the darkness of this mother's world. The deep ache in my chest began to lessen just a bit as I filled the paper. If there was one thing I was good at, it was mobilizing people to get behind a cause. This was definitely a cause, and I became filled with hope as I imagined God's people in action in the life of this woman.

Now before I go on, I want to ask you something, because this is important.

Of all the things that I wrote down on that piece of paper, what do you think was the very first thing that I did? They were all great ideas, and all of them would help this woman and her children, but I believe that where we start is very important. So this is a good question.

Go on; hazard a guess.

What did I do before anything else?

Sometimes I have told this story when speaking to a group, and usually when I ask this question, someone calls out, "Prayer!"

Great answer.

I wish it had been mine.

No, I didn't start with prayer, although I'd like to think that my time spent writing furiously on that paper and conversing with God qualifies as prayer.

If it wasn't prayer, what do you think I did first?

I'll tell you. I did absolutely nothing.

I don't mean that I did absolutely nothing, and *then* I got started. I mean I did absolutely nothing.

Ever.

Kind of disappointing, even shocking, that this is the punch line for the story, isn't it? At this point I wouldn't be surprised if you're wondering why you are even reading this book. I wouldn't even be shocked if you started looking for the receipt—as long as none of the pages are dog-eared, you could probably still take it back.

I am not proud of the way I responded. But I tell you this because maybe, just maybe, you might recognize yourself in this story. Maybe there has been a time in your life when you saw a need, were deeply affected by it, and *meant* to do something.

Intentions are wonderful things. They are the starting points, the defining moments of our lives. But in and of themselves, intentions are wholly inadequate.

As a Christ follower, it's easy to mistake intention for action and stirrings for solutions. I sometimes give myself credit for being a pretty remarkable human being just because I feel angry about injustice, pain over suffering, or empathy in the face of hurt. But even the strength of my intentions is not an accurate indicator of whether or not I will take the time to act, to put my faith to work, to be the difference that Christ has empowered me to be.

Defining moments are only as good as the lifestyles they translate into.

I have reflected many times on that day and those intentions I had to help this family. I'm still not sure what happened. I drove home that night, eager to tell my family what I had experienced in that home in Baldwin Park, filled with hopeful thoughts and feelings about the difference that we could make. That list rode shotgun in the car all that next week. I looked at it often, from time to time adding to the action items, making mental notes about the people I needed to call to help with the list. A few days later, in a hurry somewhere, I tossed a couple of books and a purse on top of it. Even as that next week wore on, however, the list always found a way to surface to the top of whatever I dropped on it. But then someone rode in my car with me, so I tossed the stuff from the front passenger seat into the back. I made a mental note to dig out the list as soon as I could. And I meant to. But then some newspapers were added to the backseat pile, and then one day, I think it was at the car wash, I emptied the contents of my car into the trash can without thinking.

So what was it? Was it selfishness? busyness? Was I paralyzed by the scope of the need? The answer is probably yes—to all of the above. But now, years after the event, my best thinking on it is this: *It matters how you live.*

I had a great opportunity and great ideas. I could have

done some great things for that family. I *should* have done some great things for that family. That day, God had caused my workday to intersect with this family's need. What could possibly have been more important than responding? When I first made that list, I wanted to do everything on it. Now, years later, I wish I would have done at least one thing on it.

Sometimes we find God in our failures. Our painful, embarrassing, public failures. Trouble is, often when something hurts, we avoid it. And when we do, we pull away from the very thing we need to face in order to encounter God.

I have gotten to the point in my life where I am rarely surprised by my sin, just saddened by it. Surprise indicates that I did not think I was capable of such wrongdoing. I now know that is rarely the case.

Sadness helps me understand my need for Jesus. Sadness at my thoughts, behaviors, actions—or lack thereof.

Sadness helps me understand that without Him, I am lost.

12

DON'TFORGETTO REMEMBER

As I write this, July 4 is just around the corner. Summer is in full swing, and we will soon add to that the requisite backyard BBQ of hamburgers, hot dogs, and corn on the cob. The smell of warm grass, the taste of summer fruit, the feeling of cool water in a swimming pool all declare that summer is officially here.

These same sights and smells always transport me back to my childhood and my grandmother's house, where all the cousins and aunts and uncles gathered every summer for the

Fourth of July celebration. I can still feel that carefree spirit of youth, the sweat on my skin as we raced around the backyard, and the anticipation of homemade ice cream. Every year, we would eat watermelon until our bellies were bloated and follow up with a scoop of vanilla ice cream, the sweetness melting into our mouths as we turned our faces toward the sparkling colored lights exploding in the sky above.

These are not simply wonderful memories. They are something much deeper. These memories remind me of a time when I felt safe and free to drink in the goodness of life. There is bedrock in these memories.

I love to go on a journey of remembering the sights and smells and tastes and joys of my childhood celebrations. But if I continue on that journey beyond those initial superficial memories, I can reach a much deeper place: a place where there is a direct connection with God, the Creator of all sights and smells and tastes and joys. That freedom and joy I felt in my grandmother's backyard is more than just ice cream and games with my cousins. In reality, it is a connection to God and His character. His universe is a reflection of Himself, and it is filled with all these good things. That is bedrock. And that is where remembering can take us.

I would like to live every day of my life in that same sense of freedom and joy I had when I was seven. But as an adult, I tell myself this is impossible because life is much more complicated than it was when I was a child. That is true. But it's just as true that God is the same God He was on July 4, 1962.

Certainly my life is more complex than it was in 1962. Certainly I've faced many difficulties and hardships since then. And yet, the same freedom and joy are available in God's universe. I just have a short memory.

I live, as Wallace Stegner wrote, where I can see the last sunset on the continent, just a short twenty-five minutes from the Pacific Ocean. I often go there to walk along the beach. It may be one of the most centering and filling things that I do. It is always amazing to me that the water and waves I see have traveled thousands of miles from a distant land to wash up on my shore. There is something about being there, seeing the bigness of God and feeling that I am safe in His hands, that helps me put everything in perspective.

When I am at home, it's easy to forget what I experienced at the ocean. Even ten minutes into my drive home, with the ocean at my back, I can lose my centeredness and per-spective. I have a short memory. The funny thing is, I know the ocean is still there, with its rhythm and its message. I'm the one who has forgotten.

The power of remembering transcends its evocative na-ture. It is about more than simply recollecting or reliving. Remembering pulls the past, with all of God's presence, into our present and our future. At its best, it reconnects us to God and His activity in our lives. Remembering puts things into perspective, reminds us that God was present, acted mightily in our lives before, and promises to do it again. It reminds us, when we remember.

Remembering is like looking in the rearview mirror. Most of the time when we are driving it is a good idea to be looking forward. Every once in a while, however, a glance in the rearview mirror at what's behind us is also a good idea. Sometimes what is behind can tell us a lot about where we are going and how we should proceed. A glance behind can inform and mature us, ready and deepen us for what is next. The view that shows us God's faithfulness readies us for what lies ahead.

Remembering is, in large part, what makes us human. Certainly as we get older our ability to remember is somewhat curtailed, but isn't it amazing that we can reach into some forgotten recess of our brain and retrieve a memory that transports us to another place and time? In an instant the sights, sounds, and smells that surrounded a particular moment are brought to life. As we remember, it is as though the event is actually happening again.

Of all of our senses, perhaps smell has the most evocative ability. Helen Keller, who was both blind and deaf, said this about smell:

> Smell is a potent wizard that transports us across thousands of miles and all the years we have lived. The odors of fruits

waft me to my southern home, to my childhood frolics in the peach orchard. Other odors, instantaneous and fleeting, cause my heart to dilate joyously or contract with remembered grief. Even as I think of smells, my nose is full of scents that start awake sweet memories of summers gone and ripening fields far away.

Strange that odor molecules are able to make their way through the air and into the nose to interact with the more than five million olfactory cells residing there. And in doing so, a few maverick molecules remain connected to a darkened corner of the mind, ready to revive our memories with just a whiff.

I am fifty years old, and to this day the smell of pineapple juice immediately reminds me of preschool snack time. A sniff of hay reminds me of my horse-training days, and the pungent odor of salmon eggs has me on the banks of the Black River, trout fishing with my dad.

A few years ago my husband decided to try wearing a new aftershave. The scent was nice, but, I told him, unless you want me thinking about another guy I used to date every time I smell it, you had better go back to Pierre Cardin. I didn't mean to think about that guy, it was as if my brain was on autopilot.

In her book *A Natural History of the Senses*, Diane Ackerman calls smell "the mute sense." She writes,

Nothing is more memorable than a smell. . . . Smells detonate softly in our memory like poignant land mines, hidden under the weedy mass of many years and experiences.

The physiological links between the smell and language centers of the brain are pitifully weak. Not so the links between the smell and the memory centers, a route that carries us nimbly across time and distance.

The act of remembering is so powerful—and smell is one of the more remarkable ways that those distant memories are awakened—that God reminds us often to do it. The Old Testament is full of stories and stone altars and incense, all of which are intended to find the brain pocket that contains a particular memory and stir it. Not only is the Old Testament full of this advice, but when Jesus ate His final meal with the disciples He ended the meal with the admonition to remember Him every time they repeated the experience.

God often called His people to remember, but His people have short memories. And while sometimes certain seasons or smells or sounds can prompt remembering in rather unexpected ways, we can be intentional about remembering. We can do it on purpose.

On the first anniversary of September 11, we created an Axis service called "Don't Forget to Remember." The service was beautiful. One of our interns put together a powerful video of images from September 11, which was accompanied by Fernando Ortega's haunting song taken from Psalm 32. As we sang in worship, we pleaded with God to hear us and intervene in our broken and messed up world. Scripture passages flashed on the screen, reminding us of the importance and power of remembering. Then I gave a brief minisermon called "Don't Forget to Remember."

We ended the evening with more singing and an invitation for people to come to the front of the room. About ten Axis staff members and volunteers lined up along the stage, and as scores of people filed forward, we tied pieces of string around their fingers. Then we prayed for them and told them, "Don't forget to remember."

One of the people in my line was a twenty-three-year-old girl named Jen. Jen had been a part of Axis for three years and was on the music and production team. She was very bright and worked as an engineer for a large company, but she also struggled deeply with depression.

Jen had been in and out of treatment clinics, tried different medications and counselors, and attempted suicide twice. Her small group had been an amazing support during these difficult times, but Jen's depression was relentless. I was glad that she was in my line, because I liked her a lot.

I tied the string around Jen's left forefinger, prayed a quiet prayer over her, and then said, "Don't forget to remember, Jen." When she looked up at me, her eyes were filled with tears. She pulled me close and whispered, in response to something I had said in my message, "Is it true? Is He really close, even in the hard times?"

I whispered back, "Yes, Jen, especially in the hard times."

It was a touching and sweet moment.

The next week Jen arrived before the Axis service to work with the setup production team. As I was moving around the gymnasium checking with different people in preparation for that evening's service, Jen made a point to find me. She told me she wanted to show me something. Just seeing her reminded me of our interaction from the week before, but her face looked happy, and I was glad for that.

Jen said she had been to a tattoo parlor that week. At first I wasn't quite sure how to respond to that, but she looked so happy I figured it had to be a good thing. Then she pushed up her sleeves.

Jen's wrists still bore the evidence of her failed suicide attempts. But now, tattooed on the inside of each wrist, right on top of those slash marks, was a word I didn't recognize. I held Jen's wrists in my hands and looked intently.

"It's the Hebrew word for 'grace,'" she said. "Every time I looked at my wrists before, I could only remember the desperation I had felt. I wanted to remember the presence of God, who was there during it all. And the string kept coming off my finger. This doesn't come off."

I just stared for a moment, unable to take my eyes off those scars and that beautiful Hebrew word for "grace." Unbelievable.

Who would have thought that our memories could be devotional? Objects in mirror are closer than they appear.

Indeed.

13
MODEL

THERE IS A WORD I would like to see expunged from the lips of Christians: the word *model*. And I am not talking about Tyra Banks.

Most often it is used in the context of leadership, but even beyond that, Christians are often told that we need to model the behavior and lifestyle that God wants. Pardon me for hairsplitting here, but I think when we use the word *model* in that way, we move people dangerously close to living incongruent lives. And heaven knows we have seen enough newspaper stories about Christians falling into that.

Model implies that regardless of what we believe or feel or think on the inside, we should at least try to make the outside look good. This way of thinking causes us to live externally, for others, rather than internally, out of a center that is connected to God. It moves us toward unhealthy compartmentalization when we say one thing but do or believe something else entirely. Always in secret though, so no one sees that the two sides don't match up.

The word *model* is only used three times in Scripture. That's pretty amazing when you think about how often we talk about it. Ezekiel 28 uses this word to describe the king of Tyre. Although he was eventually corrupted by pride and violence, this ruler started out pretty well: "You were the model of perfection, full of wisdom and perfect in beauty" (Ezekiel 28:12). The word is not being used here to suggest that we emulate the king of Tyre, since it's clear that he does not hold on to that status when sin pries its way in.

The other instances of the word are found in 1 Thessalonians 1:7 and 2 Thessalonians 3:9. In 2 Thessalonians, Paul says he, Silas, and Timothy were models for the early Christians to follow. They modeled hard work, laboring and toiling so as not to become a financial burden on the people in Thessalonica.

In 1 Thessalonians, Paul writes about these same people in the church in Thessalonica: "And so you became a model to all the believers in Macedonia and Achaia. The Lord's message rang out from you not only in Macedonia and Achaia—your faith in God has become known everywhere" (1:7-8). Paul was commending their lives of faith, not a behavioral modification program they were on for the sake of others. Early in that chapter Paul describes the way they received this renowned faith with these words: "Our gospel came to you not simply with words, but also with power, with the Holy Spirit and with deep conviction" (verse 5).

Their modeling was not simply external behaviors that masked a different internal reality. They modeled the power of the gospel that had resulted in deep life change, and their faith was known in all the surrounding areas.

A more congruous way to talk about modeling is to talk about authenticity. There is a great difference between those who say we need to model Christian behavior for others, and those who live so well with God that people ask them about their faith. We want to live in a way that others would like to model, because we really believe this is the way to live deeply with God. We live it because we believe it, not because we feel the pressure of others watching.

Authenticity means being honest about our struggles, knowing that in that honesty, God will meet us and transform us. We want our insides and our outsides to match. I am drawn to people like that. And I think that is what God had in mind for us as His followers. People who live deeply with Him are magnetic. They are winsome and brave and courageous and open and honest and real. That is modeling based on the power of the gospel, which transforms lives.

In his book *Generating Hope*, Jimmy Long writes about two conversions as people decide to follow God. First, he explains, there is the conversion to community, and then the conversion to God. Many times, people aren't able or willing to make the leap to God right away, and it might take long-term exposure to Christian community before they are drawn toward the God who is at the center of that community.

This was certainly true of the early church. In Acts chapter 2, the community of believers is described as devoting themselves to teaching about Jesus, having meals together, praying together, and selling what they had in order to provide for those who didn't have enough. They were joyful and had sincere hearts, and as a result, they "enjoy[ed] the favor of all the people" (verse 47). *The Message* translates it this way: "People in general liked what they saw."

The result: "The Lord added to their number daily those who were being saved."

The greatest apologetic, the best defense or evidence of our faith, is the way we live authentically with God. Authenticity implies honesty, struggles, questions, desert times, shaking fists, and hopeful silences. I can only model what I am experiencing. Anything else is either behavioral modification or "faking it"—neither of which is transformational.

We have this mistaken idea that living the Christian life is a series of mountaintops, a succession of grand faith adventures.

It is not.

Some people live in such an attractive way that I am compelled to watch. There is grace and poise, joy and hope, sorrow and pain, mistakes and distance—all with God. Those who have the courage to do so are rare, and they should be our models.

God lives in the struggle. It is there we find Him.

14
HEROES

I WONDER IF WE ARE LOOKING in the wrong places for our heroes.

I wonder if we have brought the celebrity culture home to our churches.

I wonder what it would look like if, at the next Christian conference you attended, those who spoke hadn't built a megachurch or written a book.

If Jesus came to Glendora, California, I think He would stop at the house of Babs Conklin and have something good to say about her. But I'm not sure Babs has ever been asked to speak at a church conference.

Our loss.

Babs is a wife and a mother of three. I often wonder where she gets all of her patience and if I might be able to buy some of it. She is a kindergarten teacher, so you'd think she would spend all of her patience at school. But she comes home with it too.

This past year, Babs donated her left kidney to a man who needed it. He wasn't a relative or even a friend. He was a friend of a friend. Babs heard that he was on dialysis for hours each week and that his only hope was a kidney transplant. So Babs went to be tested to see if she might be a match, and she was.

Then Babs told her family what she was going to do. Her husband went to the doctor's appointments with her to listen to the risks and what they could expect. And then he went with her to the hospital on the day of the transplant. He waited while they operated on his wife and removed one of her kidneys. He was in the waiting room when the surgeons came out to tell him Babs was doing well and that the man who needed the kidney had turned from gray to pink within minutes of receiving his new kidney.

Now Babs is recovering, and the man is free from dialysis and from the fear of impending death.

If you see some brother or sister in need and have the means to do something about it but turn a cold shoulder and do nothing, what happens to God's love?

—1 JOHN 3:17, *The Message*

Love can be such a difficult word to define. Except when a kidney is involved.

Dave and Shirley attend our church. They have been married for almost forty years and have raised three kids. They also take in infants, providing temporary care until the babies can either be placed back with their parents or into long-term foster care or adoption. They might only get an hour's notice before a baby is dropped off, and then they might care for that infant for four hours or up to three months. Sometimes when I run into Dave and Shirley at church, it's just Dave and Shirley. Sometimes when I see them, it's Dave and Shirley plus a baby or two. You just never know.

In almost forty years of marriage, Dave and Shirley have taken in more than eighty babies. You should see their faces when they have one of those babies. You'd think someone was doing them a favor.

Every day, behind the scenes and without any fanfare, Christ followers are doing something heroic. They are people who have been deeply loved by God and can't help but give to others. People whose stories make you want to sit a little straighter, dig a little deeper, and give a little more. These people inspire the deepest parts of me, the parts that are connected to God. I'm not inspired by the way they look or what they have written. I'm inspired by the way they love.

It is desperately important to our faith that we choose the right people to be our heroes. And in order to do that, we have to look in the right places.

Jesus turned Roman centurions, women, lepers, and children into heroes. He saw what most overlooked. He was not looking at the way these people dressed or what they built. He looked at the way they loved and the way they trusted, their gratitude and the simplicity of their faith.

Real heroes lift our heads. They stir those places deep inside each of us that ache for meaning and significance and purpose and God. Real heroes remind us that love isn't that difficult to define.

A man in our church is one of my heroes. I can't put his name in this book, because I know he'd die of embarrassment. And he might even sue me to keep me from doing that.

But anyway, this man is a pretty successful businessman and a great family man. He travels a fair amount and has worked for years to keep his faith alive and practical and transformational.

Every Saturday he goes to the bank and withdraws a "wad" of fifty- and one-hundred-dollar bills. He puts them in his wallet and whispers a prayer that God will nudge him during his travels. Through that practice, he's realized that most hotel housekeepers work for minimum wage. So he always leaves a generous tip on his pillow when he checks out of a hotel. In addition to the tip, he offers another whispered prayer, asking God to bless the lives of the people who have kept his room tidied during his stay.

Last month, when this man was in Colorado, he took a few minutes to have his shoes shined in the hotel lobby. He struck up a conversation with the man doing the work and discovered that this man had just arrived from Mexico three days prior. He was here on a six-month work visa, sending the majority of his money home to his wife and four children. It was his second day on the job.

My friend leaned down and told him, "Since you are just starting this job, I don't want you to think many people will do this, but please accept this, along with my prayers for you and your family." As he spoke, he handed the man three one-hundred-dollar bills. That story moved me so deeply, I still pray for that man who shined shoes.

Larry Clark is another one of my heroes. Larry was an unusual man, maybe even quirky. Yes, Larry was definitely quirky.

On a staff of about eight, ministering to the "eighteen to twentysomething generation," Larry stood out as a full-time volunteer who was about forty years old. Larry came to our staff meetings, had an office in one of our cubicles, and just poured his life out into the leaders of this ministry.

Larry had worked for a number of years at IBM and had left with a small nest egg after opting for an early retirement package they offered in order to downsize. He supplemented his meager income by being a substitute teacher a few days each month, and he gave, quite literally, over forty hours a week to our ministry. He was passionate about discipleship and leadership development. He would often identify a handful of eager—or at least curious—young adults in our ministry and spend hours teaching them and bringing them to events where they could be exposed to inspired teaching and interactive learning. He mailed them books he thought might speak to their unique season and circumstance. He sent them tapes and CDs to listen to in the car and took them out for meals, talking to them about who they were, who God was, and how those two intersected.

Larry once said, "I am an artist, and my canvas is people."

When I first started working in Axis, I quickly realized that nearly everyone there had some kind of connection with Larry. That was a bit confusing because I expected someone with that kind of influence to be a pretty impressive person—at least in the ways I often think of as impressive.

Did I mention that Larry was quirky? When Larry was on the phone with one of his protégés, he usually talked really loudly. And since he was in a cubicle, everyone around him got to hear the conversations. It became something of a joke among our staff. One day one of the staff members got up on his chair and pointed a bullhorn at Larry when he was on the phone, shouting, "Larry! Can you talk a little louder?"

Larry fell off his chair and started laughing until tears rolled down his face. He never did talk more quietly though. I think his exuberance and passion just came out in high volume. At staff meetings he was always excited about the spiritual growth of someone he was working with, and his words could barely keep up with his brain as he tried to tell us about it.

Larry lived on very little. He didn't seem to think about things the way others did. He lived in a small apartment, and when we had Axis staff lunches at church, he often packaged up the leftovers to ease his budget for the week. Actually, Larry often packaged up the leftovers from other staff meetings in the church as well. Once, when I asked Larry how he managed to eat enough on his sparse income, his face just lit up. He said, "You would not believe what you can get out of the trash bins in the back of the grocery stores after midnight!"

I probably wouldn't.

Once I gave Larry a staff bonus check of fifty dollars, along with a note thanking him for all he did in our ministry. You would have thought I had bought him a house.

Larry deeply invested in the lives of others, but he didn't

seek the spotlight for himself. It wasn't that he was uncomfortable with the spotlight, he just didn't even notice if it was pointing toward or away from him. His joy came from the work he did, work that didn't pay.

In the fall of 1999, our church sponsored a retreat, and about three thousand people who were involved in the small-group structure gathered in Milwaukee, Wisconsin, for two days of worship, community, teaching, and vision. A large contingency from Axis stayed together at one of the many hotels in the area. The first morning of the retreat, I was eating breakfast with a group of Axis leaders when Heather, one of our staff members, found me. Heather told me Larry had been in an accident. She was pretty calm, and from what she knew at that point Larry was alert and talking, so it didn't seem to be too bad.

As we walked together to the scene, Heather relayed that Larry had been up early that morning, jogging with four or five of the guys he discipled. Toward the end of the run, Larry insisted that the young guys run ahead.

"I'm right behind you, just go ahead," he had said. And shortly after that, Larry stepped off a curb and was hit by a city bus. By the time we arrived at the scene, the ambulance had left with Larry, but what was left in the street made me realize that things were *not* okay. The fire department was working quickly to wash blood and bits of skin and bones off the streets.

Daniel, another Axis staffer, and I jumped in his car and headed to the emergency room. Dan McFarland, one of the guys Larry had been running with, was there to meet us. He had been in the ambulance with Larry on the ride to the hospital.

"It doesn't look good" was the first thing he said.

Shortly after that the doctor came out to tell us that Larry had died.

Apparently I wasn't the only one who had considered Larry to be a hero.

For the rest of that day and well into the evening, we stayed at the emergency room while young people from Axis poured into that place. They came in disbelief, in grief, and in love. Many of them waited in shifts while three and four at a time went in to see Larry's body. For some, it was the first time they had seen a dead body, but they all wanted to see Larry.

No one wanted to leave. We all just wanted to talk about Larry. About how giving he was, and how present and attentive he was. About his contagious enthusiasm for God, and about his servant's heart. Larry had embodied the word *servant*.

Some talked about the book, tape, and CD collections they had amassed, thanks to Larry. And others talked about the long conversations they had had with him. Everyone talked about the way he had listened and encouraged and remembered. We laughed together as we talked about how quirky he was and how loudly he talked.

Later that evening, when we all should have been in bed, the Axis group gathered in one of the hotel meeting rooms and sat in an enormous circle, continuing to talk about Larry. He had obviously affected many lives—deeply. The stories just poured out of people. We couldn't stop talking about what a remarkably unique person Larry was. How he chose to live his life in heroic ways, wrapped around meaning and significance and God. Unfettered from money and status and ego.

A few days later I stood next to Larry's family who had flown up from Texas for the wake. Eight hundred people waited in line to pay their respects, and each had a story to tell. The variety of people in that line was testament to Larry's eclectic reach. One elderly woman with neatly coiffed white hair and wearing a suit and gloves shook my hand. When I asked her how she knew Larry she whispered, "Well, dear, I don't usually pick up hitchhikers, but . . ."

A few of the Axis guys cleaned out Larry's apartment before the funeral. On his desk, they found the fifty-dollar check I had sent him. A Post-it note was stuck to the check, with the name of someone he had planned to give it to. Larry must have figured that guy really needed it.

That weekend in Axis we dedicated an entire service to this man who had lived among us. We called it "A Life Well Lived." That was Larry.

During the service, I asked everyone in the room who had been directly impacted by Larry to stand: anyone who had been in one of his Bible studies or who had had one of those long, formative spiritual conversations with him. Anyone who had a growing library because of Larry. Scores of people stood to their feet. I asked them to remain standing. Then I asked those still seated to look at those who were standing. If their life had been directly impacted by anyone they saw standing, would they also stand?

Nearly half of the room stood. And as we looked around, a collective, quiet gasp could be heard across the room.

One quirky guy.

A life well lived.

The ripples move out, the artist keeps painting, and people are changed.

Dallas Willard says that God does not spotlight His special ones. Jesus came in a way so unobtrusive that many missed Him. Perhaps our heroes aren't in obvious places. Perhaps we will have to train our eyes and our hearts and our minds to find them.

I promise it will be worth the effort.

15

OPENORCLOSED

YOU CAN TELL A LOT about people by looking at their hands. When I was a little girl, one of the things I loved best about my dad was his hands. They were pretty rugged and competent, and they gave away the fact that he was an avid outdoorsman. When I went fishing with him, his hands always communicated that he knew exactly what he was doing.

Dad would stand by the creek and pull the test line out of his reel. With quick dexterity, he would slip the line through the guides on the rod, thread a beaded lead weight onto it, close it around the line with needle-nose pliers, tie on a hook, bait, set, and cast the line in a seemingly single motion.

We often hunted together too. I have a picture of me at three years old, wearing a flannel shirt tucked into my jeans, with a hunting dog by my side and a 410 shotgun under my arm. Dad wanted a boy. He didn't get one, so he made do. When we finished hunting for the day, my dad stood out among the hunters due to his ability to clean and dress the birds we shot with quick, easy movements, in record time. I will spare you the details, but as a kid, I was pretty impressed.

Just so you know, not only was my dad an avid outdoorsman, he was also a principled sportsman. He set few rules, but one was nonnegotiable: you shoot it, you eat it. Once my cousins and I were out in the desert with my dad and my uncles hunting for rabbit. During a lull, we kids decided to shoot at lizards. Long story short, even with ketchup, lizards don't taste like chicken.

Whether they held a fishing rod, a shotgun, or a golf club, my dad's hands had a kind of masterful familiarity.

Recently one of my daughters told me that I had my mother's hands. I think her exact words were, "Mom! You have Grandma's hands!" And before I could thank her for the observation, she launched into the detail supporting her hypothesis: thready veins that pop up, brown age spots, and thin, loose skin. Out of the mouths of babes . . .

You can tell a lot about people by their hands.

When it comes to our hands, we have a choice. We can either go through life with them closed: tightfisted, fearful, angry, reluctant, withholding, comparative, and empty.

Or we can go through life with our hands open: generous, expressive, grateful, helping, and full.

The way we hold our hands reveals a lot about our hearts. And the way we perceive the posture of God's hands tells you a lot about *His* heart. In fact, we can extrapolate an entire theology based on how someone sees God's hands.

I think I spent a lot of years thinking God's hands were closed.

I think I was wrong.

James 1:17 says, "Every good and perfect gift is from above, coming down from the Father." So from the time we wake up in the morning until we lay our heads back down at night, everything that crosses our paths—especially everything that is good and brings us joy—is from God. That couldn't happen if His hands were closed.

In Psalm 104:24-28, David practically trips over his words trying to describe the goodness of God:

> How many are your works, O LORD!
> In wisdom you made them all; the earth is full of your
> creatures.

There is the sea, vast and spacious, teeming with creatures
beyond number—living things both large and small.

There the ships go to and fro, and the leviathan, which you
formed to frolic there.
These all look to you to give them their food at the proper
time.
When you give it to them, they gather it up;
when you open your hand, they are satisfied with good things.
(EMPHASIS ADDED)

God's hands are open, and from them tumbles every good
thing. And those good things give us an inside look at the
nature of God. His open hands point us to His generosity
and compassion.

Luke tells the story about someone whose hands were
pretty tightly closed. But after he met Jesus, that all
changed.

Zacchaeus is not just a flannelgraph kids' story, although
many of us think the main point of this story is that he was
short and had to climb a tree to see Jesus.

Luke starts the story off by telling us that Jesus was enter-
ing Jericho.

Very important part of the story.

Jericho was important in Palestine. From its location,
Jericho commanded the approach to Jerusalem from the

east as well as the crossing of the Jordan from the west. Trade and commerce passed through this busy, populated, and wealthy city. That's the setting.

The main character is a Jewish man named Zacchaeus. If you grew up going to Sunday school, you probably can't help humming "and a wee little man was he." But being short was not the most important thing about Zacchaeus. Right after Luke introduces Zacchaeus, he lets us know that this man was the chief tax collector and very wealthy.

For a writer of that day to say that Zacchaeus was the chief tax collector *and* that he was wealthy was completely unnecessary. If he was the former, he was definitely the latter. Back in those times, the tax system lent itself to gross abuses. The Roman government, which ruled over the land of Palestine, would assess a district at a certain figure and then sell the rights to collect the taxes to the highest bidder. As long as the assessed figure was paid at the end of the year, the bidder was free to keep whatever he collected above that amount. Most often, the tax collectors were Jewish men who were viewed as traitors by their fellow citizens.

Now you can see why the people of that day put robbers, murderers, and tax collectors in the same category. Tax collectors were banned from the synagogue. They were not well liked. Okay, they were pretty much despised. In fact, it was common for "average Joes" to exact revenge by bumping, poking, and bruising tax collectors when they appeared in crowds. So in addition to Zacchaeus's being short, this was probably one of the main reasons he wanted to avoid the crowd when he went to see Jesus.

In fact, Luke 19:4 says that he ran ahead and climbed a tree. He wasn't even around the crowds; he was ahead of them. So there Zacchaeus was, sitting up in the tree—away from the people who despised him and protected from the elbows of those he collected from—waiting for Jesus.

Now for just a second, let's go to the end of the story, where Jesus said that He had come to save what was lost (Luke 19:10). From Jesus' perspective, Zacchaeus was lost. He had closed, tightfisted hands that unfairly collected taxes from the people and kept great wealth for himself. All of those things qualified Zacchaeus for the "lost" category.

And at some level, I think Zacchaeus already knew that. He was willing to brave the crowds (okay, I know hiding up in the tree wasn't exactly brave, but at least he was out there) for a chance to see Jesus. Zacchaeus was successful, but he wasn't fulfilled. He was wealthy, but he wasn't happy.

We are meant to live with our hands like God's hands, not like Zacchaeus's.

Living in Jericho, Zacchaeus must have heard stories about Jesus. Luke tells us that he wanted to see Jesus, so something must have prompted that. He must have heard rumors that this new, unorthodox rabbi was telling stories that turned the outcast into the hero. Maybe he had heard the story Jesus had told about the Good Samaritan. *A Samaritan? Are you kidding me?* Jesus took a guy the Jewish people hated and made him the hero of the story. Zacchaeus knew what it meant to be hated. But he'd never been the hero of a story. Now Jesus had his attention.

Someone probably also shared another story Jesus had told about a rich guy who was throwing a party (Luke 14). Zacchaeus was rich, and he had thrown a few parties in his time. He was all ears.

When no one accepted the rich man's invitation—which was unheard of in that day, by the way—the host told his servants to bring in people who were poor, handicapped, and blind. Then he sent them out again to the far outskirts of the town so they could invite even those who lived far away. He wanted his party to be full.

A rich guy opening his home to the very people everyone else avoided? It's no wonder Zacchaeus wanted to see who Jesus was.

And apparently, Jesus wanted to see Zacchaeus, too. He stopped at the tree in which Zacchaeus was perched and told him that He would very much like to go to Zacchaeus's house right then. Who knows what stories Jesus told when He got there, but by the time Jesus was ready to leave, Zacchaeus's hands had opened.

Here's what he said:

> Look, Lord! Here and now I give half of my possessions to the poor, and if I have cheated anybody out of anything, I will pay back four times the amount.

LUKE 19:18

That was Zacchaeus's spontaneous response to having been with Jesus. Being with Jesus somehow relaxed Zacchaeus's grip and opened his hands to pour out generosity on those who didn't have as much, probably many of whom he had collected taxes from. Believe me, tax collectors back then would *never* promise to make fourfold restitution *and* give away half of what they had.

I think we make Zacchaeus's story a children's story because if we don't, it has huge implications for us. *Give away half?* Maybe it's better to focus on the tree and how short Zacchaeus was instead.

But if we take this story off the flannelgraph board, there is so much for us to see. God's hands are flung open, and there is no end to His generosity, His compassion, His good things. His hands are open, and if we live in a trusting relationship with Him, our hands can be open too. We can grow our hearts by opening our hands.

When our kids were little, we intentionally tried to teach them (and ourselves at the same time) to live with their hands open. Every once in a while, we would call the kids over to the desk where we paid the bills, and we would show them the tithe check, explaining what it was and why we did it. We told them this was where our giving began but not where it ended. Then we would turn it over and ask them each to sign their names on the back of the check. It was a small way for them to participate with us in this important practice.

This past summer, a friend of mine told me about his family's summer vacation. He and his wife have four children, all teenagers, and they are quickly getting to that stage in life where family vacations are rare. This year, they were able to spend ten days together traveling, hiking, seeing movies, eating out, and enjoying conversations together. It was a great vacation, and my friend was so grateful for the experience.

On the plane ride home, his sixteen-year-old son sat next to him, just beaming. He asked his dad to get out a piece of paper.

"Dad, let's list everything we did on vacation and how much it cost," he said. My friend was not at all sure where this was going, but he went along with the boy's request. When they finished the list, his son looked him in the eye and said, "Dad, let's save this same amount of money up and give it to a family that can't afford a trip like this."

Goodness is compelling. Being blessed creates a sense of gratitude. And gratitude moves us toward giving, our hands opening until they look like God's hands.

We are not the end of the line, not cul-de-sac recipients of God's goodness. We should be like sieves: God pours through us so that we can give to others. Two hands—both open—one with which to receive, the other with which to give.

Our churches and our lives should be epicenters of generosity. Our relationship with the God of the open hand prompts extravagant and sacrificial generosity. Every prison, nursing home, AIDS clinic, and school within a thirty-mile radius of our churches and our homes ought to be overflowing with volunteers: all God's people with hands that are flung open.

In this past year, John and I visited two different families that were new to our church. Both families had young children, and both had fathers who were critically ill.

One family lost the father about a week after our visit; the other dad continues to live in a chronic state of ill health that prevents him from being able to participate in the family to any significant extent. Our visits were sobering.

But during our visits, both families mentioned people from our church who had already been there and were delivering compassionate, ongoing care and assistance. Even though John and I got word very early on about these families, we were not the first ones there. Others, moved by the circumstances, were already present.

Just last week I spoke with a friend at our church whose

twenty-year-old daughter is hospitalized with a serious condition that will most likely require intense treatments and a bone marrow transplant. I asked what we could do to help, and she referred me to a woman at our church who was already coordinating meals and other help.

Already there. Already with open hands. So like God.

Every time God opens His hands, good things tumble out. Not just good things for our benefit but good things that tell us about a good God. Good things to show us how good it is for us, too, to live with open hands.

Two thousand years ago God's hand opened once again. And into the still quiet of the night a baby was born in a stable. His cry pierced the night, and the world was never the same. Because once that baby was born, the Cross was inevitable.

The ultimate opening of God's hand.

16

LONGINGS, ACHES, AND PAINS

One of my favorite places to hike is a mountain trail near our home. At the top, on the days I make it that far, is a stunning panoramic view of the San Francisco Bay on one side and the coastal hills on the other. After hiking through groves of oak and eucalyptus, I emerge at this vista of the bay, sweeping up to the hills and skyline of the city. Turning my face just slightly, I can see the redwood-covered coastal hills that separate us from the Pacific Ocean. It is a magnificent view.

The last time I hiked the trail, I stood at the top of the

mountain and took it all in. Feelings of joy and contentment flooded over me as I looked out at the view. It was a
warm day with brilliant sunshine, and the hike had been
invigorating. My body felt strong and challenged, my eyes
were drinking in the sights, and my heart felt alive and
happy. From time to time during the hike I had reflected
on the people and circumstances that graced my life, and I
was thankful to God for all of it.

But then, I felt something else. Something very different
from what I just described.

An ache, maybe.

Just a little one.

This feeling had a wistful quality to it. A poignancy that
was bittersweet.

It felt like a slight breeze or a far-off train whistle you
could sense more than hear. It was buried in everything else,
but it was there nevertheless. I found myself shifting my
stance, as though doing something physical might quiet it.

Although it was small, I wondered if the reason I noticed
it was because it was such a contrast to the experience I had
been having. A little disruption to the warm feelings, a dis-
traction that might go away if I just left it alone.

And leave it alone is what I often hear. In the name of
following God, I am told to focus on the good stuff. Even
though doing so seems inauthentic to me. I am applauded
when I speak in terms of blessings and power. But people

nervously shift and move to change the subject when I mention that things are sometimes difficult and that something might be wrong with me.

But I think there is—something wrong with me, that is.

And the ironic thing is, God is so often the most real to me when I go to those difficult places. Yet I want to avoid them, and quiet them, and pretend they are not real.

When John and I moved to the Chicago area to be a part of the staff of Willow Creek Community Church, we were both excited for the opportunity. It was a wonderful era in our lives, and we raised our children there for the bulk of their school years. The work that we were doing and the people we were doing it with were remarkable.

But for me, living in Chicago was really difficult.

I am a native Californian. A native Southern Californian. Second generation. Grew up with a dad who believed the outdoors was everything. I fished in the rivers, lakes, and sea with my dad. I rode my bike through our neighborhood and through the open fields of eucalyptus trees that we kids called "The Jungle." Most of the time, I wore nothing but shorts, a T-shirt, and flip-flops.

As a child, I spent every day outdoors where orange trees and palm trees grew together. The air was warm, and the topography of the land was rich with the texture of hills and valleys and mountains. The ocean was thirty minutes west, and the mountains were an hour east. California was an outdoor paradise that deeply shaped who I was, although I didn't know to what extent until I moved away.

Suddenly I was living in a place where people wore layers. And they wore them most of the year. From mid-October until mid-May, Chicago was cold and we needed to keep our windows and doors shut. If we pitched a tent in our backyard in the middle of the winter and slept outside in thin sleeping bags, we would die.

Leaves fell off of the trees, and for days and weeks at a time, the sun did not appear. The land was unrelievedly flat, as if God had taken an iron and pressed out all of the bumps. To me, it felt like death. Chicago convinced me that hell would be cold, not hot. I hated it.

Don't get me wrong. A lot of good stuff was going on during this time in my life. I was tempted to bury this non-life-threatening struggle in the middle of all the good things. The good outweighed the bad, so why not just focus on that?

But for most of my life, I have met God most deeply in the middle of the hard stuff. I didn't know much, but I knew that. So instead of burying it, I chose to face it and pay attention to it. I chose to wrestle with it and try to listen. And I chose to live with it and all the tension and sadness it produced.

I don't think God moved me to Chicago to teach me this, but since He had me there, it was as good a time as any to ferret this out. I spent time alone, allowing those thoughts and feelings to bubble up rather than pushing them down.

When someone asked how I was doing, rather than giving them a smile and saying, "Doing fine, how about you?" I started talking with people who could help me in grappling with my feelings.

I found that God met me in my sadness. I found that the deep ache and longing I had for California was also a reflection of being an alien in this world. Not fully belonging yet longing to. Being created for a perfect world but living in one that is imperfect. The spiritual layers became more available to me as I dug a little deeper and allowed the longings, aches, and pains to have their voice.

And when I did, what slowly emerged was a growing phrase from God: *You love California more than you love me.*

Well, maybe, but just a little bit. Is that a problem?

I began to understand what "idolatry of place" was. I found friends who weren't afraid to engage me in conversation, reflection, and challenges about my own idolatry of place. I discovered that God was a strong place I could go to when the sense of loss felt overwhelming. Through this process, I realized that God is the one thing that can never be taken away from me, the one thing that doesn't change. And that understanding became the center of who I was.

This issue of my idolatry was not monumental. It was not life altering; no one was dying or making poor choices. It was not a "defining moment." But even in some of the lesser issues, we can meet God in such profound ways. Ways that develop Him as bedrock in our lives. Ways that make His strength and presence palpable. Ways that cause us to create a well-worn path to God that forms the center of who we are.

Every longing is an echo, an ache for the perfection that we were created in the image of. If we pay attention to the pain, struggle with it and live in it, we grow. We know God more deeply. He is more real to us and intersects our lives. We understand how we can apply the love of God and the power of the Cross to our lives.

If we ignore the longings and cover them over with platitudes about blessings, we lose. We miss the chance to apply God to our lives. He becomes a cliché and we, a joke.

Two of the most powerful things that God offers us are His grace and His forgiveness. Yet when we insist on ignoring the difficult parts of life, we are effectively saying that we don't need those two things. So the power of God is lost in our lives. And we wonder why following Him has become predictable and dull.

When my first daughter went away to college I gave her a gift when we left her in her dorm room. It was a journal—but not just any journal. It was a "mistake journal." I told her that each night before she went to bed, she should write down three mistakes she made that day. I said that as long as she was going to write them down, she might as well write down the big ones.

Then, after recording them, she should take that journal,

slip it under her pillow or onto her bedside table, and fall asleep knowing that the earth was still spinning on its axis, God was still in control and loving her, and tomorrow was another day. While I'm not advocating mistakes for the sake of mistakes, there is something very powerful about dispelling fear by realizing that your mistakes are not stronger than God's love for you.

That realization builds a strong central core in your soul that is unshakeable.

If we face them, our longings, aches, and pains take us to an alone place. Perhaps that is why we avoid them. But if we refuse to avoid them, we find what is true about the alone place.

That it isn't alone.

In John 16, we read about Jesus walking His disciples through their growing realization of His imminent death. This was not how they had pictured it all ending. Jesus acknowledged their grief and then told them of the coming of His Holy Spirit (verse 7). Jesus told them that soon—within days—they would all scatter and leave Him alone. Facing death and the disciples' abandonment, Jesus understood what it meant to be alone.

> You will leave me all alone. Yet I am not alone, for my Father is with me.
>
> JOHN 16:32

My Father is with me. That is what the alone place can teach us if we let it. That is what we can experience in our longings, aches, and pains if we do not run from them.

We all have black holes in our souls that keep anything from filling us up for too long. They keep us in a constant state of neediness, always seeking reinforcement through pleasure and comfort and busyness. But if we allow ourselves to experience the longing, refusing easy answers for the aches and pains, we'll slowly build solid bedrock of God in our souls. Those alone places create a foundation that closes up the black hole for good.

We all need to hear God's voice. Our longings, aches, and pains are thin threads to that voice. Stay long enough in the aloneness, and you'll find that the silence of God becomes a whisper, and then the whisper becomes the voice that you recognize.

Our willingness—or lack thereof—to wait determines if we will follow the threads or cut them. Waiting is not the same as doing nothing. If we wait well we allow God to do His work in us, to shape us, to connect to us, and to soften our hearts and our minds. Waiting well reminds us that we are not alone, but that the Father is always with us.

About a year ago, a man in our Wednesday evening home study group shared something he was struggling with. We all listened, and when he was finished, some in the group spoke to him about the issue, about himself, and about God. And then one of the women in the group said, "I think we all so want to help ease this and give you an easy answer. We want relief for you. There may be things that God wants us to say to you along the way, but beyond that, I think the best gift we can give to you is to let you know that we will be with you as you walk with God through this struggle."

She encouraged him to face the issue, not ignore, avoid, or drown it out. She talked about being willing to wrestle with God, and to take the pain head-on rather than trying to numb it through destructive behaviors. To listen, to search, to struggle, and to wait.

It was kind of a quiet, holy moment. We all knew that this woman spoke from experience. She had emerged from the alone place, not unscathed, but certainly connected to God in a way that we all envied.

We all have those—longings, aches, and pains. Sometimes they come in seasons, sometimes in waves. Sometimes they are fleeting and momentary. Sometimes, chronic and lifelong. They whisper and gnaw, they pester and annoy, they explode and recede. And in the end, they may be the very deepest point of connection we can have with God. We are not alone.

My first response is rarely to listen to the ache, give voice to the longing, or sit still with the pain. I move quickly to dismiss and ignore them, distract myself from them, or excuse them. Slowly, however, I am learning that if I pay attention to them, these threads will take me back to God.

Picture yourself with a wheelbarrow filled with all of your longings, aches, and pains. You might be tempted to push it around to anyone or anything that will quiet them. Satisfied for the moment, you move on, lost to the fact that you are still pushing around a wheelbarrow.

But what would happen if we all took our wheelbarrows to God? Pushing that load of dissatisfaction straight to the heart of the One who knows what we're really about? If we did that, God could begin building a strong core in our centers, a core made up entirely of Him.

The more we push our wheelbarrows toward the center of ourselves where God lives, the more familiar the path becomes. It gets easier to find the more times we use it. When we allow God to build our core around Him, that core becomes our identity in Christ. And suddenly, at least for the moment, there are no wheelbarrows.

I know a young couple that wants desperately to have a child. They have been married for about eight years and have spent the last three trying to get pregnant. At first, they went about it the good old-fashioned way. But as the months went on, they were surprised to learn that it wasn't as easy as they had hoped. After a while, what had begun as a desire for children turned into a longing. And then that longing gave way to an ache, and the ache took root and grew into pain.

They've been to doctors, spent huge amounts of money, and endured the physical discomfort of shots and hormonal fluctuations—all of which have taken their toll. Month after month, they have experienced the heart-wrenching disappointment of another lost opportunity to be parents.

The last time I ran into them, however, they looked different, happy. I immediately thought the obvious but for once didn't blurt out what I was thinking. They seemed eager to tell me what had happened.

No pregnancy . . . yet. They were still committed and hopeful in the process. But their happiness stemmed from something else. They had just financially helped another infertile couple to adopt a baby. They had heard about this couple from someone in their church. The couple had been through several *near* adoptions, and this one looked very promising. But they were out of money. And my friends were not.

As I listened to them talk about what they had done, I was quite stunned. In the middle of their pain, how was it possible to reach out so generously to another couple, giving that couple what they themselves most wanted?

They both talked about how open and honest and raw they had been with each other and with God. They sat still in their pain, at least some of the time, and realized that they were not alone. And when they met this other couple, they decided to donate funds to secure an adoption for them.

"I know people will say that *we* could adopt, and maybe someday we will come to that decision," the husband told me. "For now, we remain focused on trying to get pregnant, and we're hoping that will happen."

The husband went on to say that as they prayed together about their desire for a baby, this idea to help someone else emerged. "Believe me," he said, "I wouldn't have thought this one up on my own. But as soon as we decided to do it, it was like this joy flooded our sad situation. I know this isn't a promise of a baby for us, but it is the promise of the presence of God in such joy."

Every once in a while, I find myself speechless—usually when I am overwhelmed. What this couple had done was remarkable. This sacrifice was a thread that they clutched and followed all the way back to God. It was also a wheelbarrow set down.

Henri Nouwen wrote that we have nothing to offer others if we don't know that we are loved by God. Of all the places we go to get love, our longings, aches, and pains are the most powerful and convincing. If we have the courage to go there and to live there in healthy ways, we will surely find that healing awaits us.

17

ALLINEED

QUINN STARTED ATTENDING AXIS when he was about twenty-four. A group of guys that he hung out with had invited him, and he was pretty unsure about the whole thing at first.

Quinn was warm, engaging, and quick-witted. He was really fun to be around, and he quickly connected with the folks at Axis. Even at twenty-four, Quinn was doing quite well financially, but he seemed to really struggle with the issue of money as it related to our faith. Almost every time he spent time with people from Axis, Quinn would eventually get around to asking, "So what about that 10 percent tithing stuff? Do you guys really do that?"

I'll bet Quinn asked that question for nearly a year. I think he was really surprised how many people his age tithed regularly. These were people just like him, following Jesus not just because it was how they had been raised or because they were looking for some kind of eternal ticket. These people followed Jesus to the point of being sold out for him, which included voluntary and joyful giving of their own money.

Jesus talked about money—a lot. He made it very clear that our attitudes toward money directly reflect the conditions of our hearts. The more we cling to our money and call it *ours* and the more we accumulate and mindlessly spend, the weaker our connection to God becomes. Those attitudes are driven by fear and self-centeredness.

Jesus said that it is very difficult to both be rich and follow God. Now when we read those words, it's easy to assume that He's talking about "other rich people." We all know people wealthier than we are, so we tell ourselves this passage really doesn't have much to say to us.

But compared to 95 percent of the world's population, every one of you reading this book is inordinately wealthy. I am too. This passage has much to say to us.

The fear and self-centeredness, the greed and self-sufficiency, the arrogance and pride that fuel our warped perspectives on money also reflect our misunderstanding of the nature of God. But when we understand the truth about His goodness and abundance, His care and His gifts, we can't help but have a right relationship with our money.

In Genesis 33, we read the story of Jacob and Esau, two brothers who were reunited after many years of estrangement. When they first saw each other, Jacob went on ahead of his traveling party and bowed down seven times as he approached his brother. Jacob's response was a sign of honor, forgiveness, and repentance.

Esau's response was more spontaneous. He ran to meet Jacob and embraced him, threw his arms around his neck, and kissed him. They both wept at that point. After years apart, any hard feelings and feelings of betrayal were now a distant memory, pale in comparison to the joy of being reunited.

In anticipation of their reconciliation, Jacob had brought his brother a present. At first, Esau declined the gift: *No really, I can't . . . you shouldn't have.* But Jacob responded, "Accept this gift from me . . . for God has been gracious to me and I have all I need." So Esau accepted it.

When was the last time you thought, *God has been gracious to me and I have all I need?*

Maybe this is the way you always think, but for most of us, our eyes are usually focused on what we don't have. Most days, our culture bombards us with all the things we "need" to *get*, things that are bigger, better, and more advanced. In our never-ending ascent up the ladder of success, we find ourselves spending what we don't have to acquire what we only think we need.

God has been gracious to me and I have all I need.

I know followers of Christ who really get this. I am inspired by the way they live their lives. They intentionally live on less than what they make, and they don't attempt to keep up with anyone. They are satisfied and content, filled with joy and freedom—just the opposite of what you'd expect from someone who doesn't have much in terms of material things. They limit their spending and give reflexively. They first tithe to their churches, and then they support organizations and individuals who are extending Christ's Kingdom in this world. They feed the poor, supply medicine to the sick, and support those who use their gifts to compel others toward God.

One family I know is paying for their cleaning lady's daughter to go to college. Another family lives in a rather affluent neighborhood but does much of their shopping and business in a nearby, less affluent community. Not only do they support the businesses this way, they have also come to know many of the workers in those places on a first-name basis. This practice has kept the family grounded and grateful and reminds them that not everyone has the resources to live in a nice, safe place or to feed their family on a regular basis.

I know another mom who also lives in a very affluent neighborhood. She has three children in elementary school and has always been very active in their classrooms. But last year she stopped being a room mom. Here's what she told her kids:

"Just a few miles from here live families who are pretty poor. Many of the kids live with only one of their parents, and sometimes their moms or dads have to work two jobs in order to make enough money to keep their apartments and feed their kids. Many of the kids there don't have new backpacks or shoes every year like you do, and the ones they have often have holes in them. There are gangs in their neighborhoods, and the kids there are afraid to play outside.

"Your school has plenty of moms and dads who help in the classes, but in this town, the parents can't do that. I would like to go help in those classrooms. I will miss working in yours, but I hope you can understand why I want to do this."

Her children's eyes welled with tears. They nodded vigorously, as the tears spilled down their cheeks. Over the next few nights, when she tucked her kids into bed, they peppered her with questions about this world just a few miles away, where children weren't safe.

After she had spent some time in the nearby neighborhood school, this mom began to bring her kids as well. They made friends with some of the students there, and soon their money followed. Kids' allowance money combined with their parents' checks provided backpacks and shoes and classroom supplies.

This young mom is raising three fine young adults-to-be who are learning to follow God with their time and their money and their joy and their passion. I know it is tempting to read this and either feel guilty or simply try to reproduce these same actions in your own life. Don't.

We all have to follow God out of our own stories. We can be inspired by someone else's story, but ultimately we follow God when we listen to Him speak to us in the context of our own lives.

Each of these families or individuals started in a different place. And that's why they can sustain what they are doing. That's why there is so much joy and freedom in the way they live. They began by challenging their misconceptions of God and their own fear and self-focus. And then they made life changes starting from the inside and working their way out.

Real faith emerges when we give serious consideration to our attitudes toward money. The grip that money has on our lives will determine the amount of freedom we experience.

And the level of mindfulness we apply toward our finances will be reflected in the way we see—or don't see—a generous God who is the source of every good gift.

18

HOLY

I've never much cared for the word *holy*. A lot of other words that describe God—*loving, powerful, omnipresent*—I'm good with.

Holy. That one has always been hard for me. It has always made God seem so distant, a bit angry, even "holier-than-thou." I know what you're thinking, but still.

And it's not a word we use much, except when we are talking about God or swearing.

Sometime right around February 1990 I changed how I

felt about that word. For a number of months we had known my dad was dying—pancreatic cancer. He had wasted down to ninety pounds and was turning yellow. Although he had fought valiantly, there came a point when we knew there would be no winning. A very wise person told me, "Now it's time to help him die well."

February 14 is Valentine's Day, and February 16 is my parents' wedding anniversary. My dad died on February 15. Mom called and said that the nurses had told her to call us, so my husband and I got to the hospital around 6 p.m. It was not the first time we had gotten a call like that, but as soon as we made it to his room, we knew it would be the last.

Mom was exhausted from hours at his bedside—hours that had come at the end of an eighteen-month battle with cancer. We told her to go home for a while and that we would stay with Dad.

He was semiconscious for the first hour or so, and I used the opportunity to talk into his ear, mostly telling him things I remembered about growing up as his daughter. I definitely reminded him about the lizards.

After a couple of hours, he slipped into a coma and stopped responding to my touch and voice. His breathing changed, and his hands and feet started getting cold. As his body began to prepare for death, my dad lost control of his bowels. A nurse came in to clean him up, and I stepped to the back of the room. She was so gentle with him, even though she knew he couldn't feel anything, draping the sheet carefully to protect his dignity, even in those last moments.

But as she pulled the sheet back slightly, I caught a glimpse of his back and leg. He was skeletal, and his skin was yellow. The room smelled bad. It was all so wrong.

Rather than reaching the acceptance phase of this death and dying thing—after all, it *had* been eighteen months—I just wanted to scream about how wrong this all was. This was not the way it was supposed to be. He was sixty-two years old. He was planning to take an early retirement, and he and my mom were going to travel. He was the grandfather of a four-and-a-half-year-old, a three-year-old, and a one-year-old. Yet here he was, fifteen minutes from death in a body that had deteriorated so much he was nearly unrecognizable.

That's when it hit me. Holiness, whether I liked it or not, was what I craved. A holy world, a world set right, the way it was supposed to be. Sacred and pure, clean and strong. A holy world, where there is no smog in LA, no cracks in the sidewalk. A holy world where children are never hungry, wars are never fought. No snow in Chicago, no struggles that overtake us, no fathers dying.

Holy.

Holy, holy, holy. I may never fully understand the word, and it may never be my favorite descriptor of God, but now when I sing about it, I mean it. There is a sense of longing in the word now, a longing that defines the word in a way that makes me nod. There is an ache in that word now. Because of the pain, *holy* no longer feels distant or angry or superior. It is a soft, kind word, a word full of promise and hope. A word that cannot be fully realized until there is no death.

19

REAL

ONE SPRING WE HELD an Axis retreat, and hundreds of young adults gathered at a center a couple of hours away from the church. It was my first retreat as the Axis leader, and I really wanted to communicate well and share deep teaching and inspiring vision.

On Saturday night, I gave a quick message after dinner, and then we held a worship concert. The place was packed, the lights were dimmed, and the music was loud and passionate. It resembled a rock concert, and that isn't all bad.

People couldn't get enough, and the clamor for more pushed the music and singing late into the night.

Being the only person over forty in the room, I told my staff I was going to my room to go to bed. If anything got out of hand, they should feel free to wake me up. The concert went on for at least another hour.

The next morning at breakfast, bleary-eyed but enthusiastic, many of the attendees were still talking about how great the worship had been.

But I had a very different take on it.

When I got up to speak, I started like this:

"Something happened here in this room last night, there's no doubt about it. There was an incredible amount of energy and enthusiasm and response. Some are calling it worship. I'm not yet convinced.

"When the day comes that this community has the same amount of energy, enthusiasm, and responsiveness for the poor, the marginalized, and those far away from God and each other, then I will believe that what I witnessed last night was worship.

"Until then, I think what we saw last night was a compartmentalized emotional catharsis, which while it might have been enjoyable, was *not* worship in any sense of the word."

Worship is a whole life response to God. It is not just about singing, or even about getting caught up in the singing. Those are not bad things in and of themselves, but they are not complete in any way. That night, I observed hundreds of people getting caught up in the way the singing made them feel, even though many of them were divorced from God in most other areas of their lives.

Perhaps I recognized it because I've done it myself.

When we are not living a real faith, we are tempted to fake it. If my insides aren't experiencing it, at least I can make my outside fall in line. But faking it only results in more of the same, rather than real transformation. It results in a distancing from God and a misunderstanding of who He really is. And the cycle starts all over again.

In Isaiah 29:13 God is once again frustrated with his people. They have done it again. They have done what the Pharisees would do hundreds of years into the future. They have done what you and I are still doing today.

> These people come near to me with their mouth and honor me with their lips, but their hearts are far from me. Their worship of me is made up only of rules taught by men.

This worship is only on the outside. Religion deteriorated into behavioral modification. No connection between the lips and the heart, between the rules and the mind. External actions often lull us into believing that we are pleasing God, while our hearts and our minds remain unconvinced. And that way of living falsely paints a picture of a God who asks for that. So we follow a God who allows for this gap, and we wonder why we are not amazed and astounded by Him.

In Matthew 23, Jesus has a pretty direct confrontation with some of the misguided religious leaders of His day. You would think that when the Messiah showed up, the first people He'd talk to would be the religious powers that be. And He did, but He didn't like what He found. He told the crowds who had gathered to hear Him that the teachers of the law and the Pharisees did not practice what they preached and therefore should not be imitated. No wonder Jesus had such crowds gathered around him. They had never heard this kind of message before.

Jesus went on to give examples of the way the Pharisees did everything for other people to see. They followed all the cumbersome rules of religiosity, but they themselves were not transformed.

On the outside, they dressed well, sat at the honored seat in public places, reveled in being called Rabbi, and followed religious protocol down to the detail of tithing on their spice gardens. I wonder if Jesus was frustrated with them because as representatives of God, they had so misrepresented God. In verse 25 Jesus sums up what was wrong with what they were doing: "You clean the outside of the cup and dish, but inside they are full of greed and self-indulgence."

Religion can tempt us to do a little behavioral modification on ourselves. Internal transformation can be so much work and so difficult to measure that it is easier to just clean up and conform on the outside. But all that work on the outside can fool us into thinking that the inside is being taken care of as well.

I am capable of being angry and impatient on the inside yet conciliatory and sweet on the outside.

I am capable of treating God like a stranger on the inside but acting as if I know and follow Him on the outside.

I am capable of being jealous and envious on the inside but humble and gracious on the outside.

I am capable of, well, you get the picture. Religion gone wrong, the religion that many of the Pharisees adhered to, says that if it is too tough to change the inside, just work on the outside. Get that really shiny and gleaming. And don't pay any attention to the gnawing sense that something isn't quite right.

It's easy to think, *Well, I may struggle with jealousy, envy, and impatience, but at least it's not adultery and murder.* But Jesus said, "Inside they are full of greed and self-indulgence."

Greed and self-indulgence. That's what Jesus got so worked up about? Couldn't He do better than that? At least He could have accused them of some A-list sins. You know, the ones I *never* commit. This chapter in Matthew is filled with name-calling. Jesus compared the Pharisees to blind fools, hypocrites, and snakes. He was angry. But you'd think He would have saved this level of anger for something newsworthy.

If He had criticized the Pharisees for something like child abuse or assault with a deadly weapon, I could stand and nod my head in agreement, then shake it side to side to show my disappointment in their behavior. I could convince myself that Jesus' criticism of the Pharisees had absolutely nothing to do with me. I could even feel a little superior, which is such a delicious feeling. But I can't get away from greed and self-indulgence.

God's vision for restoring and reconciling people to Him is not about behavioral modification or an outside cleanup. It is about an internal heart change that reflects the heart of God. It's a lot more work than the outside stuff, but there is something compelling about understanding that God is much more interested in the integrity of my heart than He is in a good-looking exterior.

In Matthew 23:26, Jesus went on to say, "First clean the inside of the cup and dish, and then the outside also will be clean." His prescription for changing what is wrong has nothing to do with working on the outside. In fact, Jesus says that by cleaning the inside, the outside will take care of itself.

So, whenever I sense that my inside and outside don't match, I know it's time to dive deep into my heart and line up its darkness with the glorious nature of God. That's where transformation has its power. Not in my own effort, but in who God is. Certainly I do not sit idly by while God works His magic, but my effort helps only when it brings me to the God who does the transforming. And much of the transforming lies in my correct understanding of the nature of God.

In order to experience true transformation, I need to decide what I believe and why I believe it. Then I need to figure out a way to live according to those beliefs.

I am better equipped to live out a faith that is real when I have wrestled and read and thought and prayed about what I really believe. *Who is God? How is He different from what I have thought? What is His true nature?*

And, in light of who God is, how shall I spend my days and my resources? In my money, in my relationships, in my responses, in my time, in my work, in the care of my body and mind, in my conversations, in my silence, in my driving, in my falling asleep and waking up. How do I watch TV and read books and water my lawn and be a neighbor and pay my bills and answer my kids and read my Bible and be a great employee?

How can knowing who God is inform each moment of my day, each choice that I make? And when I lose sight of that knowledge, can His love and forgiveness free me from beating myself up and help me see that tomorrow is as fresh as His mercies?

If I spend my time considering who God is—His faithfulness, His love, His forgiveness, His grace, His holiness,

His righteousness, His redemption, and His radical inclusion, just for starters—I am prompted, no, I am compelled to live in light of that.

Reconverted

20

STARTSAND**STOPS**

THERE IS SOMETHING about beginnings and endings that is clarifying. Beginnings hold the promise of hope, the expectation of the new and fresh. They are a chance to start over or anticipate. The first cry of a newborn, just-bought school supplies in September, the start of a day as the sun peeks in. Opening a book to chapter one, meeting someone for the first time when you "just know" that this friendship will be pivotal. Emerging from the car wash, Mondays, and forgiveness—all bring belief in the possibility of renewal.

God is in beginnings. *In the beginning God created . . .* one of the ultimate acts of hope. When we create or when we participate in beginnings, we sense God. We learn something about Him, know Him more deeply. We reflect His nature in those moments. The hope and renewal has its source in Him.

In the beginning was the Word, and the Word was God. *In the beginning.* In between beginnings and endings, life happens . . . but beginnings, they give us hope. They give us clarity around the simple things that loom most important.

Extraordinary acuity.

When I worked as a nurse, I witnessed death on a regular basis. The process of dying is not clean and quick like it's portrayed in the movies. It's slow, destructive, relentless, and ugly. It smells, and it tortures.

Nearly thirty years ago, I stood by the bed of a patient who had just died. I had seen patients die when I was in training, but this was *my* patient. His name was Mr. Barth, he was ninety-one years old, and he was from Russia. The nurse who was training me saw the look on my face.

"First patient that died?" he asked.

I nodded.

"Don't ever get over the sadness I see on your face right now."

I nodded again.

I took that moment very seriously. Mr. Barth had died

just a few minutes after I started my shift that day. He had been my patient for three days. As I had taken care of Mr. Barth, we had chatted some, and I'd found him to be winsome and charming. He was elderly, but had clarity and a sparkle in his eye that reminded me that it was his body, not his soul, that was old. He had told me a bit about growing up in Russia, and now as I stood at his bedside, with his body still and cold, I wondered who his parents had been and what he had been like as a little boy and a young man. I wondered about his hopes and dreams and how he ended up dying in Orange, California, in 1978.

On the other side of beginnings are endings. Endings teach us *how* to begin, what we should center our lives upon, and what is really important. Life has to be grounded in things that can never die, can't be stolen, and can't get taken away.

Endings have a purifying effect. When the dust settles after a crisis hits, we can find what is real—what is core—by what is left behind and who rose to the occasion. Endings strip us down to that.

When the final breath leaves the lips, and the soul—that which infused the body with life—and the body are separated, it is clear which was the more important. Ecclesiastes says that we all "share a common destiny. . . . The same destiny overtakes all" (9:2-3). The end may be just the right starting place.

When my dad died, I stood by his open casket at the visitation. I wanted to place a few photographs of me and my family inside his inner suit pocket, and as I bent down to reach into his pocket, I was surprised by the strong scent of formaldehyde and the stiffness of his body.

This was not my dad. My dad had been so fully alive. He embraced life and filled a room. He had exuberance and energy. He golfed and fished and hunted and worked and laughed and bantered. And when he was alive, I thought that was mostly his body. But I was wrong. I still had his body, but I did not have him.

His soul—the part of him that responded to a voice, followed a stirring, made his heart race and filled his mind with glorious thoughts, the part that gave him a sure step and a confident look—had left him as surely as his last breath.

In some ways, his soul was at its most magnificent in the end when he was suffering from terminal cancer. We saw it in the confident courage he displayed when he drove alone in his red Mustang to his radiation and chemo treatments. We saw it in the impudent hope with which he walked around the block to gain strength when the disease had wasted his six-foot frame to a hundred pounds.

My soul had lifted and swelled at the sight of him.

He didn't want the end, even when the end promised an ease to his suffering. He didn't want the end because he wasn't done with life. He didn't want the end because souls were not made for endings. . . .

Eternity is written in beginnings and in endings. It is written in the souls of others and in the space between us. Jacob, after dreaming one night of God and promises and eternity, awoke to say,

"Surely the LORD is in this place, and I was not aware of it."

Surely.

ABOUTTHEAUTHOR

NANCY ORTBERG served as a teaching pastor for eight years at Willow Creek Community Church in South Barrington, Illinois. During that time she led the Network ministry, helping people identify their spiritual gifts and find a place of service in the church.

She also led Axis, for the eighteen to twentysomething generation. Axis included weekend services of 1200–1500 people in their twenties who worshipped together, served the poor, and participated in small group communities.

Nancy is a founding partner of Teamworx2, a consulting firm that works with organizations, helping leaders overcome the team dysfunctions that are obstacles to high performance and work enjoyment. She and her husband, John, live in the Bay Area and have three children, Laura, Mallory, and John.

NOTES

20 *"The acid test for any theology"* Dallas Willard, *The Divine Conspiracy* (San Francisco: HarperCollins, 1998), 329.

53 *"Even with his body"* Aleksandr Solzhenitsyn, *One Day in the Life of Ivan Denisovich* (New York: Penguin Books, 1963).

93 *Jesus is actually like a Warhead* A few years ago in Axis, Don Everts was our special speaker. Don has written a book called *Jesus with Dirty Feet.* This thin little book makes the Gospels come alive, as a gritty, real-life Jesus seems to jump off the pages at you. During his time with us, Don used the Warheads illustration to make this same point about Jesus' intensity and power.

95 *"A Jewish man was traveling"* Luke 10:30-32, NLT

96 *"Then a despised Samaritan came along"* Luke 10:33-35, NLT

114 *"Nothing is more memorable"* Diane Ackerman, *A Natural History of the Senses* (New York: Random House, 1990), 5, 7.

183 *"Surely the LORD is in this place"* Genesis 28:16